T0247728

Hero Me Not

Hero Me Not

• •

The Containment of the Most Powerful Black, Female Superhero

CHESYA BURKE

Rutgers University Press

New Brunswick, Camden, and Newark, New Jersey

London and Oxford, UK

Rutgers University Press is a department of Rutgers, The State University of New Jersey, one of the leading public research universities in the nation. By publishing worldwide, it furthers the University's mission of dedication to excellence in teaching, scholarship, research, and clinical care.

Library of Congress Cataloging-in-Publication Data

Names: Burke, Chesya, author.
Title: Hero me not : the containment of the most powerful black, female superhero / Chesya Burke.
Description: New Brunswick, New Jersey : Rutgers University Press, [2023] | Includes bibliographical references and index.
Identifiers: LCCN 2022028672 | ISBN 9781978821057 (paperback) | ISBN 9781978821064 (hardcover) | ISBN 9781978821071 (epub) | ISBN 9781978821095 (pdf)
Subjects: LCSH: Storm (Fictitious character) | Women superheroes. | Superheroes, Black. | Women, Black, in popular culture. | Comic books, strips, etc.—United States—History and criticism.
Classification: LCC PN6728.S755 B87 2023 | DDC 741.5/973—dc23/eng/20220902
LC record available at https://lccn.loc.gov/2022028672

A British Cataloging-in-Publication record for this book is available from the British Library.

Copyright © 2023 by Chesya Burke
All rights reserved

No part of this book may be reproduced or utilized in any form or by any means, electronic or mechanical, or by any information storage and retrieval system, without written permission from the publisher. Please contact Rutgers University Press, 106 Somerset Street, New Brunswick, NJ 08901. The only exception to this prohibition is "fair use" as defined by U.S. copyright law.

References to internet websites (URLs) were accurate at the time of writing. Neither the author nor Rutgers University Press is responsible for URLs that may have expired or changed since the manuscript was prepared.

♾ The paper used in this publication meets the requirements of the American National Standard for Information Sciences—Permanence of Paper for Printed Library Materials, ANSI Z39.48-1992.

rutgersuniversitypress.org

Manufactured in the United States of America

I am rooting for everyone Black.

Contents

Preface

> If I didn't define myself for myself, I
> would be crunched into other people's
> fantasies for me and eaten alive. (129)
> —Audre Lorde

When actress Alexandra Shipp imagined a fully light-skinned Storm-verse in May 2019, it held the possibility of being a watershed moment for both the character and mainstream discourse around race and colorism[1] within comic universes. While the conversation around colorism is not new within comics, and not even new for Shipp and her depiction of Storm, the response was swift and almost completely negative.

The moment happens during an interview with two fellow cast members of *Dark Phoenix*, Tye Sheridan (Cyclops) and Evan Peters (Quicksilver). When asked what she would like to see in a feature film starring Storm, Shipp excitedly explains what she hopes to happen in the future for the character:

Okay, so this is what I've come up with! I think it'd be really cool if you had me and Halle [Berry] both teaming up together and fighting a baddie. We have to save the planet past, future, present and maybe throw in Yara [Shahidi] in there, and have her be a young one, or Amandla [Stenberg] be the younger one. I think it'd be even cooler. So, I feel like we just gotta get a

Alexandra Shipp's interview for Comicbook.com (Davis).

whole bunch of Storms together, because then people will just be like, "Oh my God, that's so much Storm." (B. Davis)

Clearly, Shipp has deeply pondered her own role in the franchise, however, she cannot imagine the character beyond her own physical phenotype of light skin and traditional, Eurocentric facial features. Up to this point, Shipp herself has suggested that skin tone is not important to the development of Storm as a character. Not only is this completely not true because skin tone fundamentally changes the way every individual person exists in the world,[2] but if Shipp herself believes this is true, why does she imagine only light-skinned women playing the character?

While Shipp envisions a world that has never existed in the comics, I would be remiss not to point out that Storm is written within the X-Men universe, which for all intents and purposes is a world of magic. In a world of mutants, shapeshifters, and a Black woman who can control the weather and is one of the most powerful people in the world, why is it not possible in Shipp's view that Storm can be a light-skinned child and grow up to be a dark-skinned woman—or vice versa?

Instead, as Shipp herself struggles to move beyond colorism, we are reminded how race and skin tone are wholly integral to the development of this character. Storm's race is a constant presence within the X-Men universe. The comics conceptualize her as beautiful and sexy despite her

X-Men: The Animated Series (1992). Dark-skinned Storm.

"brown skin" because "her features don't fit any conventional classification. Not Negroid, Caucasian, or Oriental—Yet somehow, an amalgam of the rarest elements of them all. White hair. Blue eyes" (Claremont 11). Another character in that same comic goes on to ask, "What's wrong with her?" (12). While Storm first appears in 1975, this quote from *Uncanny X-Men* is written in 1989 and expresses the racial tensions in which Storm has always existed. At this point in the series, they only "think [Storm is] a mutant" (12). She is considered "unclassifiable" because of her race and phenotype, and *not* because of her mutant powers.

If you think it is strange for a mainstream publication to use terms such as Negroid and Oriental as late as 1989, let me assure you that this hyper-focus on race works to cement Storm's "otherness." There is something "wrong with her" because she is not recognizably white or Asian. There is nothing in her appearance or background to suggests she is a member of either of these groups, so to suggest such is absurd. However, while her skin is clearly that of a Black person (her "Brown skin" is highlighted earlier in the text), her Blackness is classified as not "conventional" (Claremont 11). Her fair hair and complexion work effectively to distance Storm from her Blackness, placing her beyond and arguably above "regular" or "conventional" Black people. Moreover, by saying there is something "wrong" with Storm the text signals to readers that her mutant nature is not as easily hidden as for other mutants (such as Jean Grey), due in particular to her white mane and ever-changing eye color.

Uncanny X-Men #253 (1989) (Claremont).

Racialicious contributor Cheryl Lynn Eaton states that "Storm is what Black women want, or are constantly informed by the media that they *should* want but are also told that they never will achieve. To be loved and to be beautiful. To be free. To be special" (Lynn). Each woman in Shipps's Storm-verse is not only light skinned, but mixed race, with one white or non-Black parent. This should be acknowledged because despite the bizarre classifications from 1989, Storm is unambiguously Black, having both Kenyan and African American parents. Throughout her history, Storm has been depicted in various shades of brown.[3] In *X-Men: The Animated Series*, which aired from 1992 to 1997, she has dark brown skin and is voiced by Alison Sealy-Smith, a darker, brown-skinned Black woman.

In Hollywood's X-Men films, however, the normally darker-skinned Storm is played by the light-skinned Halle Berry and Alexandra Shipp.

Race is an ever-present force in Storm's life, just as it is for Black and other marginalized people. Endowment with supernatural powers has not changed Storm's position in life, though, and instead these powers have made her whiter, relegating her Blackness or "Negroid[ness]" to second-class status.

Eventually, Alexandra Shipp comes to terms with the racial and colorist dynamics around the character, stating in an interview: "In the future, I think I'd like to see a woman of darker complexion play Storm. I think it's about time that we see that representation, and I'm more than happy to see that. I think it would be really great. The little girl in me would really like to see that" (Chanliau). Whether Shipp actually believes this or said it for PR reasons as has been suggested, is unknown and it is irrelevant to the discourse here. There is no doubt, however, that there is room for the character to *grow* and develop beyond the limited depictions given both in the comics and the films.

However, "growth" does not necessitate only moving "beyond color" when the world in which we currently exist still prioritizes whiteness and proximity to it. When and if racism and white supremacy are eliminated, and representation of Black bodies is fair and balanced, then who plays Storm will become less and less irrelevant. Until then, if Storm is depicted as a light-skinned, mixed-race Black woman, she will experience the world in a fundamentally different way than the darker-skinned Black woman of the comic books. Pretending this is not true does nothing but continue the oppression of Black and marginalized women whose skin tones are darker, like that of the comic book character.

Colorism around Storm is only one of the ways in which bell hook's "white supremacist capitalist patriarchy"[4] works to impact the character (Media Education Foundation 7). In the following pages, I use personal anecdotes, pop culture and social and cultural references to hold space for Black female bodies and to deconstruct the various ways in which we have heretofore been silenced by white imaginations of powerful Black women who only use their superpowers in support of whiteness.

Hero Me Not

Hero Me Not

1

Introduction

•••••••••••••••••••••

True Blood. That was the moment all our heroes died. Well, they didn't die, exactly. Rather, as we watched Tara's Black body endure abuse after abuse even as a vampire, we realized that in fact, our heroes—those mainstream, empowered Black women figures we all love—have never truly existed. Not for those of us who matter in this conversation—Black women—and not in any meaningful way.

Some background: As a Black woman, I've had a lifelong interest in all things supernatural. From a young age, I read and reread stories of triumph such as those of Harriett Tubman and Ida B. Wells, while also devouring tales of witches, ghosts, and vampires. I am relatively certain that I was the only eight- to nine-year-old in Hopkinsville, Kentucky, that could tell you both the true history of Vlad the Impaler as Dracula and why Harriett Tubman was the real-life Moses. I devoured books, and quickly became obsessed with Storm from the X-Men and other genre works, searching desperately for any representation of Black women within them. As a child, I was interested in Storm because of her unique abilities and perceived powers. Finally, I spent so much time in the world of the supernatural that I began writing and publishing it myself. Some would argue that I became pretty good at it, being one of only a handful of Black women horror writers in the field. That's where I found myself. Developing characters that I had not seen elsewhere, yet still longing for broader representation in mainstream media.

This leads us back to the Black woman character from *True Blood*, Tara Mae Thornton (played by Rutina Westley). Fans know Tara as the fast-tongued, smart, snarky, outspoken Black woman from the long-running HBO series. Tara has been called the smartest person in Bon Temps, Louisiana, by viewers, although this is arguably not a great feat, as most of the residents are strung out on V, a highly addictive drug made from vampire blood, and the other half could easily be mistaken for such. Either way, the audience quickly realizes that Tara is different, because, well, she can read. Educational books, even. Despite an alcoholic mother who teeters between believing that her daughter is possessed by the devil and passing out drunk on a sofa, a community that often promotes the rights of vampires over those of Black women, and being unable to keep a job, Tara is empowered and surprisingly self-aware in the beginning of this often-oppressive series. In the first few seasons, Tara fights every possible enemy, both real and imagined, to maintain her dignity. The result is a flawed, lovable, but mostly autonomous character. In season five, however, Tara dies and is quickly turned into a vampire. That is the point at which Tara Thornton may very well become the only person in the True Blood series to be more subjugated as a vampire than she ever was as a human being.

The world of *True Blood* is a place that imagines itself as a post-racial paradise, and Tara Thornton is there to remind every single resident that this is not the case. Tara is aware of her position as a Black woman in the South, and in the beginning the show works very hard to never let those around her forget that she understands this. When her best friend Sookie falls for Bill, a vampire, Sookie's grandmother asks the vampire to meet with her club to discuss the Civil War. During the conversation, Tara asks Bill if he's ever owned slaves. Overwhelmed with excitement over the information that Bill's father had been a slave owner, Sookie's grandmother explains that this is exactly the kind of thing that her club would love hearing about. Disgusted, Tara asks, "About slaves?", bringing attention to the contrast between the nice airs that the group works so hard to perform in the parlor of this old-fashioned Southern house and the reality of the horrendous crimes against Black bodies that they pretend to be so far removed from. Later, at a club meeting held at a church, Sookie's grandmother calls the Civil War "The War for Southern Independence,"[1] and one of the women is so upset that Bill may be uncomfortable with the giant cross behind the

True Blood (2008). Confederate flag in church while American flag covers cross (Minahan).

pulpit that she covers it with an American flag and the club members erect a Confederate flag to complement it (*True Blood*; season 1).

In short, the fictional world of Bon Temps, Louisiana, is a place that willingly displays the Confederate flag, which has long been a symbol of hatred toward people that look like Tara, while desperately trying to avoid offending a white, male vampire with a cross—in a church. This is the place that Tara Thornton resides, and these are the people that she deals with on a day-to-day basis. Tara does not hide from the injustices in her life, though. She confronts and rejects them.

In this world, Tara is a (perhaps detrimentally) strong, independent, seemingly self-assured Black woman. Unlike the strong Black woman stereotype discussed in Chapter 2, however, she is unwilling to suffer quietly, lashing out at any perceived threat, which masks her pain and makes it difficult for many viewers to effectively sympathize with her character. Although a case can easily be made that Tara is the quintessence of the stereotypical strong Black woman.[2] Due to her sassy, sharp tongue, and in no small part to her self-education, she is empowered. When Tara's best friend's brother, Jason, is arrested, Tara marches into the police station, armed only with a limited knowledge of criminal procedure:

TARA   I assume he's been properly Mirandized. Please tell me that you informed him he has the right to have an attorney present.

DEPUTY   Maybe. Doesn't matter, though, 'cause he's got you here now.

TARA Is that funny because I'm a woman or because I'm a Black woman?
DEPUTY I thought it was funny, you know, just 'cause you can talk like a
lawyer . . . but you ain't one (*True Blood*; season 1, episode 4).

When asked how she knew all of this and whether she had been taking night classes, Tara responds: "School is just for white people looking for other white people to read to them. Figured I'd save my money and read to myself."

In this interaction, it's clear that Tara has the upper hand simply because she has empowered herself. Although it can be argued that using this power to save a white man, who has not shown her any attention despite her crush on him, is problematic, it's clear that the people in town, including the police, accept her mental superiority. This scene is an example of the way that Tara conducts herself within the True Blood world at the beginning of the series—especially when it's beneficial to white characters. Although the police have authority, and Jason himself is afraid of them, Tara does not accept that authority without question as others in the community do. She is empowered due to her own actions and knowledge of the law and not simply because she is a stereotypical strong Black woman. Notably, in the world of True Blood, one of the only other groups to have nearly enough self-awareness, intelligence, and autonomy are vampires.

We also see Tara's refusal to be a victim in her dealings with her mother. Tara understandably has a love/hate relationship with the woman, who is abusive, both mentally and physically. But Tara loves her despite everything. Even so, when in a drunken stupor Tara's mother smashes her over the head with a liquor bottle. Tara responds calmly, but defiantly: "All right. You may have carried me and nursed me, but obviously now you are set on killing me. And if I'm forced to choose between you and me . . . Guess what? You lose." Tara packs her things and moves out (*True Blood*; season 1, episode 3). She loves her mother but is unwilling to allow the woman to abuse her any longer. In this way, Tara is not contained within the four small walls in which her mother seeks to confine her, but more importantly, she is not contained by actions that are directed against her best interests. Tara's empowerment comes through her own actions and recognizing what is and is not healthy for her. Although Tara is flawed and, like many, often makes poor choices, she has the autonomy to make those choices in a series that often does not recognize[3] choice as important for women characters.

Vampires in the True Blood world are usually autonomous and have the independence to do as they please without many restrictions. Likewise, becoming a vampire is often seen as freeing. An obvious example is the character Jessica Hamby. Jessica is kidnapped by the vampire council and Bill is forced to turn her into a vampire (*True Blood*; season 1, episode 10). She is seventeen years old and, like Tara, is from an abusive home. Also, as Tara does later in the series, Jessica becomes a vampire against her will. However, despite their similarities, there is one important way that the two are different: Jessica is white, and her whiteness seems to offer her a freedom after death that Tara is not afforded.

After Bill bites Jessica and turns her into a vampire, she wakes up screaming and, naturally, scared. In an effort to calm her, he explains that she is no longer human and will forever be changed:

BILL You cannot go home. That part of your life is over.

JESSICA No more momma and daddy? No more little sisters?

BILL I'm sorry, no.

JESSICA No more belts? No more clarinets? No more home school? No more rules? Yeah! I'm a vampire!

Later she tells Bill: I don't obey anybody. Those days are over (*True Blood*; season 1, episode 11).

Although Jessica is initially afraid to die and become a vampire, she is much freer after having done so. She spends her nights in the vampire clubs, finding both sexual liberation and sustenance. In fact, at one point she is so uncontrollable that Bill tries to relinquish his job of teaching her how to be a vampire to another. When the other vampire still cannot contain her, she is sent back to Bill. Although all vampires are different, we understand that transition is often overwhelming and exciting for new vampires as they discover their new powers and the freedom that it offers them from morality.

Jessica seeks self-sovereignty in a monotonous everyday life governed by ritual, recitals, and abuse imposed by her household. Independence for her is escape from those things. In time, however, she comes to miss her family, and goes back to see them. When her father gets home, he shakes her, threateningly. After the initial shock, Jessica quickly bares her fangs, telling him: "Go ahead, Daddy. Get your belt. But this time I'll be ready for you" (*True Blood*; season 2, episode 2). It's clear through this interaction that vampirism has given Jessica more power than she previously had, in part because it confers the physical strength to fight back against her father's domination and protect herself. No longer is she the weak, submissive mortal girl; now she is in control of herself and her body. Furthermore, vampirism opens up a wide range of possibilities for Jessica that had not been available in her father's home, which allows her to shift the balance of power against him. While it may be a stretch to say that she had no control over her life before, it seems clear that being a vampire has given her more autonomy and allows her to protect herself in ways that she could not previously.

Vampirism in the True Blood world often seems to work this way. Vampires are sometimes savage and prey on humans, but they are equally protective of their own and their progeny and they sometimes show human-like emotions. There is a range of behaviors among vampires, but we rarely see them restricted or fully contained after their transformation.

That leads us to Tara Mae Thornton—and eventually, right back to Storm.

Tara becomes a vampire unwillingly, like Jessica (*True Blood*; season 5, episode 1). She dies saving Sookie's life, which she often regrets, even at one point telling another vampire that too many people have died for her long-time friend. After realizing that she does not want to live as a vampire, Tara decides to take her own life. Her maker, Pam, however, forces her not to kill herself. Suicide, it seems, is not an option for the good God-fearing folk of Bon Temps,[4] as Tara is not allowed the dignity of this release. Tara is one of my favorite characters up to this point, and I would have been sorry to see her go, but much less so if I had known what would become of her after her loss of autonomy.

After being forced to live, Tara is quickly put to work. Although in one of the first scenes of the series, Tara quits her job and punches her boss, she now bartends for Fangtasia, her vampire maker's club (*True Blood*; season 5). Tara, the self-proclaimed independent woman who can never hold a job, is now working in a small, sleazy bar without any compensation—like a slave. Later we see her dancing on a pole, wearing a two-piece leather bra and panty set, adorned with chains and a matching collar.

Of course, this dominatrix getup belies her current submissive role. She has no real power over anyone, including herself. As a viewer, we have no indication that Tara is doing these things of her own free will. Instead, we feel that she is trapped by vampirism and within the four walls of the club.

True Blood (2012). Tara as oppressed vampire (Ruscio).

She has no way out. Any time she makes a decision on her own she is commanded to rescind it by her maker, or she is publicly humiliated.[5] As a vampire, Tara has neither the freedom nor the free will she had, limited though it was, while still alive in racist Bon Temps.

Even Tara's take-no-shit attitude is contained. On several occasions she jumps up and runs out of the office when one of the other vampires enters. Viewers have not seen this demure, defeated Tara until this point in the series, and it is difficult to watch. Becoming a vampire, by all accounts, is supposed to make one fiercer and more empowered, but it has done the opposite for Tara.

At one point, Pam pulls Tara out of the bar in the full view of the crowd for claiming that the bar is "her house" (*True Blood*; season 5, episode 6). Pam does this to make it clear that Tara is a servant to the (white) vampires around her, and that she should not make the mistake of thinking that she is equal to them. Later, when an old classmate comes into the bar and calls Tara "uppity,"[6] she gets a rare opportunity to be the Tara that viewers have not seen since her pre-death days. Pam not only swoops in to put her in her place in front of a room of customers but calls her "uppity" as well (*True Blood*; season 5, episode 8). While Pam later brings Tara the offending classmate to feed on, this does not negate the public humiliation that she continues to suffer as a vampire. In fact, this suggests that she is more subjugated as a vampire, as she now has to rely on others to defend her, rather than being allowed to do it herself.

Tara gets a few opportunities to act on her own after she becomes a vampire, but even those times are not without their problems. For example, she kills the new sheriff because he is threatening her place at Pam's bar. This does little more than maintain the status quo. Pam has already declared that ownership of the bar does not extend to Tara (*True Blood*; season 5, episode 6). Tara also makes a decision to save the governor's daughter from another vampire (*True Blood*; season 5). This is out of character, as Tara did not befriend people (especially white people) when she was alive, and there seems no reason for her to have developed a particular fondness for them as a vampire. Although not friending someone does not mean that you wish to see them dead, viewers are now expected to believe that Tara is willing to risk her life for a white woman whose attitudes are not likely to differ from those held in her little, racist town of Bon Temps, Louisiana.

As a vampire, Tara feeds when Pam tells her to, she works when she's ordered to do so, and she literally dances for the amusement and entertainment of others in the club (*True Blood*; season 5). Most importantly, though, is that after she becomes a vampire Tara quickly becomes irrelevant to the plot.[7] She does not have her own storyline and any episode could continue seamlessly without her presence. This near erasure of her character and her personality is quite disturbing for fans.

The moment Tara becomes a vampire, we are in trouble. By "we," I mean every Black woman fan of speculative fiction who looks for heroes in the bodies of Black women in popular culture but can never quite find them. It would have been revolutionary to visually depict Tara as fully autonomous, coming into her own as a vampire—a Black woman with uncontrolled power. Her sharp tongue and quick wit—assisted by superpowers—could have been great assets to aid in her liberation. She was engaging enough and likable enough to garner her own storylines where she was an active participant before being a vampire. Why did this change afterward?

The "trouble" that unfolds after Tara's transformation informs the analysis that is within this book. While Tara was beholden to Pam as her "creator," all romantic plotlines involving the two of them leave Tara subjugated and wholly oppressed in ways that previous vampire characters did not experience. The series creators had every opportunity to place Tara out of Fangtasia, where she had no future, and back in Bon Temps, perhaps opening her own night spot that was more a haven to vamps and humans alike, and where she was unquestionably head honcho, the HNIC.[8] Although Fang-tasia was empowering for many people, Tara would have been freer outside of the confines of those four walls. None of this happened. By the end of the series, Tara is dead (*True Blood*; season 7, episode 1). In the end, she was treated as just a throwaway stereotype, relevant only to the white woman's character development.

So, how did we get to the year 2014, and still, a Black woman with Tara's power had to be subdued so as not to overshadow her white counterparts? Why it is so necessary for Black women to be oppressed in order for other groups to be empowered? Is there a Black woman character that is strong and powerful enough to overcome this containment and oppression?

These questions lead us back around to the beloved Ororo Munroe, also known as Storm, from the X-Men. While she can control the weather and wield it at her whim, is she powerful enough to overcome the oppression of her creators in a way that Tara, a mere Black woman vampire, could not?

What follows is a labor of love borne out of a deep appreciation for Storm and the woman she could be. It includes a profound devotion to genre fictions, comics, and all things weird and speculative, but most of all it is about love for Black women and the relentless need to find our humanity in a world that often seeks to dehumanize us.

2

Sexuality, Subjugation, and Magical Women

• •

The genre field[1] has a long history of being not only racist, but also misogynist, relying on extreme rape and violence against women as plot devices. In this way, women are rarely allowed to be the heroes of their own stories outside of the fantasy of masculinity. Although the victims sometimes seek revenge in one-dimensional pursuits of retribution, more frequently violence and other forms of racism and misogyny serve to prove the masculinity of the male protagonist or to offer him a revenge motive, even becoming a vehicle for redemptive agency for male characters. Other times these motifs are simply used for shock value. The women in these stories are often graphically raped, beaten, and murdered, as if it's necessary for the audience to experience this in great detail in order to understand the story. To further explain this, one female horror writer who prefers to remain anonymous, observed "that if a woman needs to be traumatized, lazy writers will use rape. Not as a deeply emotional growth experience, but to make the hero angry, or put the woman in her place, or to make the evil person truly appear evil. The aftermath is hardly ever dealt with." It is the case that women within these stories often do not exist as functioning, autonomous human beings, but mere placeholders for males who must swoop in to not actually protect them—after all, they have already been abused and often died horrifically for our entertainment—but to allow the men to take their rightful places as heroes.

Does this mean that rape and violence, and even racism, should never be explored within works of fiction? Of course not. In real life, however, rape is never justified, and the victims must live with the very real consequences of that experience. Although spouses, friends, and family members are often affected, we should never lose sight of where the true horror lies: in the lives of the women themselves. Women who are attacked are fully actualized human beings with dreams and aspirations and nightmares, both before and after being assaulted. Why, then, is the abuse of women so often simply used as a plot point, and why do the women who experience it so often cease to exist or become no longer important, whether physically or mentally, within these stories? Why is the journey so rarely the victim's? That is, if she is a woman. And why is she so seldom allowed to be the hero of her own story?

Viewing women as mere objects fosters an environment of hostility and harassment for women who seek representation, instead of the constructed images repetitively presented both "to" and "of" us. Accounting for the fact that racial violence/assault/rape/murder are the ultimate forms of control, it is important to examine how these constant depictions of violence impact the groups most represented as victims. In this book this means Black women, although most women should be able to find space within this analysis.

Harassment is violence. When we nurture an environment within the genre where the latter is fantasy, the former becomes acceptable in real life. I do not suggest that unwanted harassment is always racial violence/assault/ rape/murder, but racial violence/assault/rape/murder is undoubtedly the ulti-mate form of harassment. It is quite possible that genre's heavy reliance on violence against women helps to normalize the objectification and abuse of women both on and off the page and screen. This leads to societal tolerance of harassment and makes us all culpable, through our silence and muted acceptance, in these depictions of sexual and physical violence against women.

Too often the nature of the genre has fostered an ideal of male superior-ity, identity, and prowess. While none of these things are inherently wrong or bad, they have too often given rise to the subjugation of women. Fellow creators, fans, and scholars should not stop exploring the issues of violence against women. On the contrary, creators should consider the ways in which we exploit female bodies, and critically engage the ways we depict, interpret, and engage with violence against those bodies.

This book, which examines superheroes and the violence against Black women's bodies, cannot promise not to depict violence against Black women or other people. It can, however, do so in an exploratory pursuit of greater understanding of these sites of disenfranchisement and stereotypes of Black women.

This chapter will consist of two sections. The first will examine the history and importance of superheroes in our society. This section chronicles comics from their incarnation, examining how intersecting identities form these characters. The second section will look at the concepts behind stereotypes and how they impact the way we see superheroes.

Superheroes and the Impact on Black Women

Within our society superheroes have the unique distinction of being innately powerful, influential protectors. Fans often speak of wishing to be them, fearing them, and respecting them simultaneously. Superheroes are, quite frankly, the imaginary ideal reflections of society. They are the representation of the very best that we believe we can be. They exist solely for our benefit in that they are created to serve and protect our society. In short, superheroes "bring us out of ourselves and connect us with something larger than ourselves, something more universal" (Rosenberg and Canzoneri 2).

Superheroes, as we know them today, originated in comic books, which consist of graphic art panels, short sections of expositional text, and dialogue, and have evolved to include movies or television shows that use popular comic book forms, characters, or both. The comic book industry (which includes books, movies, TV shows, and other media), and thus superheroes, are a multibillion dollar a year business with a long and varied history. Although many may argue that comics reach back to European broadsheets, which debuted in the early 1600s, or more closely to Japanese manga from the 1700s, most would agree that comics as we know them today originated in the pages of *New York World* on May 5, 1895 (Petty 2).

After this debut, comics became a "mainstay of newspapers nationwide" and were mostly humorous and lighthearted (Petty 2). Soon, the themes broadened to include fantasy, adventure, and the surreal. Some of the first comics included *Little Orphan Annie*, *Buck Rogers* and *The Phantom* (Petty 2).

Due to their popularity, these comic strips, which had mostly appeared in newspapers, were expanded into their own series. The first of these saw the incarnation of Superman, and others were soon to follow, including Captain America (1941) and Wonder Woman (1941).

Each of these characters tapped into the idea of American excellence, as they fought crime and injustice both within the United States and abroad, often taking on Nazi Germany and real-world atrocities. These characters—indicative of American resilience—also banded together in difficult times to fight to keep the world safe for freedom and democracy. They were American heroes in a time of the Great Depression and were an outlet for every American, both old and newly immigrated, to find solace (Petty 3). Many are themselves gods or have gotten their powers from gods, including Wonder Woman, Thor, and Black Panther.

Initially, comic books focused on male characters, but it was not long before women were introduced. Wonder Woman was the first female comic book character to debut in 1941 around the same time as Captain America and other less famous characters who have not survived the test of time. Like many others, Wonder Woman fought for justice, peace, and freedom, but unlike other characters, she also advocates for sexual equality (Lepore). The creation of Wonder Woman has influenced the presence of women characters both within and outside of the medium.

For example, Wonder Woman's creator, William Moulton Marston, was a self-proclaimed feminist and inventor of the lie detector test. Marston states that Wonder Woman's whole story "is aimed at drawing the distinction in the minds of children and adults between love bonds and male bonds of cruelty and destruction; between submitting to a loving superior or deity and submitting to people like the Nazis" (Lepore 243). Counter to male comic book characters, Wonder Woman's creator sought to distinguish between women's sexual empowerment and subjection. Marston was a bondage aficionado, and often expressed this through images of Wonder Woman in bondage, but his ideas are influential even if the execution is arguably flawed. Wonder Woman's adventures suggest that superhero characters who are not a part of the white, male dominant class, are uniquely suited to seek out injustices that male superheroes often have no motivation to fight against. Marston's character, as a white woman without the power of the patriarchy, is an example of this.

Storm, a Black woman who first appears in the comics in 1975, is another. Although there are a small number of other Black women superheroines (such as Spectrum, Vixen, and Friction) usually only avid comic book readers can name characters other than Storm. In this way, Storm is often the only recognizable Black female superheroine and therefore is seemingly the one representative Black woman in all of the comic book, superhero world.

Rarely are positive images of Black women depicted in mainstream society and it is no different in comic books. This, like any absence of representation, seems to negate Black women's contributions to the past and present, as if we are not capable of contributing anything useful to society. It also suggests that Black women have no future within the world in which we exist and have helped to create. Whether purposely or not, the absence of Black women in the imaginary worlds of the mostly white and male dominated field of comics (fiction, film, and other mediums) has the effect of erasing and devaluing Black women in the real world, who not only do not have the opportunity to see themselves within these popular mediums, but who seek to move outside of the submissive positions that have become standard for us.

The problem is not only the negative stereotypes or submissive roles for Black women in comic books, but also that there are rarely any contrasting, positive ones. Stereotypes of Black women exist in many forms and have evolved over time. As the society has shifted, stereotypes of Black women have changed and developed. That is to say that as the society has changed, it has developed newer, more nuanced images to control Black women, and thus the stereotypes of Black women have evolved as well (Roberts 23).

Beyond stereotypes, which are an oversimplified image that can represent any group and are sometimes seemingly positive and normalized (the stereotype that Black women are strong, for example), controlling images "guide behavior toward and from those persons (being represented), constrain what is seen and believed about them, and when internalized, profoundly influence the self-perceptions of the marginalized" (Beauboeuf-Lafontant 22). Controlling images are one example of stereotypes that have a massive impact on Black women. Patricia Hill Collins, who coined the term, sought to define how these stereotypes have a prevailing effect on Black women. She states that defining and controlling the images of Black women "has been essential to the political economy of domination fostering Black women's oppression" (P. H. Collins, 142).

What follows is an exploration of controlling images as essential to the representation of Black women's lives within the media. While I am interested in the literature, I also examine the graphic images, text, and dialogue of the comic books, and the images and dialogue of several films within the ongoing series that include Storm.

Prior research has focused on controlling images for Black women, such the mammy and jezebel, but few have examined the Magical Negro in relation to Black women with supernatural powers. Black women superheroes are obviously gendered and racialized; however, their powers give the appearance that these characters are equal within the society in which they exist. It can be further argued that while race and gender oppression does exist in the comic book world, they often take a backseat to mutant oppression, and thus any oppression that Storm experiences can be attributed to mutant-phobia (fear of characters with superhuman powers). This effectively makes racism and sexism obsolete within the comic world, silencing any discussion seeking to examine its effect on characters.

Although the images of Black women have become more abundant in the media within the last few years, few of those images are positive or empowering for Black women (Entman and Rojecki 15). Likewise, there is an abundance of research on comics. However, rarely, if ever, have scholars examined the way superheroes—who often represent the ultimate powerful character seeking to right injustices within society—must navigate injustice that is racial and gendered oppression against members of their own group. As such, is Storm empowered when she fights with the X-Men to protect mankind, even though as a Black woman she is oppressed by the very system that she seeks to protect?

To that end, I look at the degree to which Storm, as a Black woman with superhero powers, is indeed empowered or subjugated within the comic world, while analyzing the graphic images, text, films, and dialogue surrounding the character.

In her 2009, article for *Bitch Magazine*, "Annals of the Black Superheroine," Anna Saini asks: What if all we knew about Black women we learned from comic books?

A further query might be: What if all we knew about empowered Black women we learned from Storm?

Superheroes and Stereotypes

While speaking to students at Yale University, Spike Lee criticized the "phenomenon" of the "magical, mystical Negro" character, which he contends "is just a reincarnation of 'the same old' stereotype or caricature of African Americans as the 'noble savage' or the 'happy slave' that has been presented in film and on television for decades" (Yale Bulletin & Calendar). The term has since become popularized as the "magical Negro" (MN), which references the stereotype of the magical Black character who is written into fiction and films to help the white protagonist on his journey, but who has no story of his own.[2] The characters are often uneducated, male, and desexualized.

Likewise, in her essay, "Keepin' It Real: A Generational Commentary on Kimberly Springer's 'Third Wave Black Feminism?'" Sheila Radford-Hill says that due to the constant negative images of Black women, Black girls find it difficult to "create self-images that liberate their spirits and ignite their creativity" (1085). One of the most damaging images, Radford-Hill admits, is of the strong Black woman. Seemingly positive, and often self-designated, the strong Black woman is self-sufficient, unnaturally emotionally strong, and seemingly empowered, thus suggesting she does not need protection from those around her or the broader society. Radford-Hill goes on to explain that "Young women are right when they say that the 'Strong black-woman' (SBW) stereotype demeans them in order to justify [Black women's] collective marginality" (Radford-Hill, 1086). Unfortunately, within the speculative genre it seems that the real-life stereotype of the strong Black woman is often conflated with the magical Negro to create a character we will call the Negro spiritual woman (NSW). My paper for *African American Cinema Through Black Lives Consciousness*, edited by Dr. Mark Reid, conceptualized the character as the "strong spiritual Black woman," but here we will redefine and critically deepen this analysis of the character, particularly in relation to Storm and mutantism.

The NSW character is endowed with magical powers that are used for the good of the broader white society, but are not enough to change her status in the world, thus keeping her subdued and contained. Furthermore, in some cases, when the comics and films do not sexualize the Black female character, the public corrects what it sees as the Black female actress moving outside of her constructed space, or being too "uppity," and sexualizes her to ensure she remains contained.

The Negro spiritual woman image should be distinguished from its predecessor, the magical Negro, because they differ in three important factors: submissiveness, mysteriousness, and sexuality. Although the magical Negro trope can include the first two, it is the third aspect that separates the NSW from the MN, its antecedent. As constructs, both images work to affirm society's ideology and current structure, but only the Negro spiritual woman image uses the sexuality of Black women to reinforce their current social status. Radford-Hill's work supports the argument that, much like the real-life strong Black woman and the magical Negro stereotypes, the NSW image justifies the marginalization of Black women as an acceptable fantasy for white society, attributes a sort of heroism to the Black woman character that does not translate to actual autonomy for her, and allows white audiences to uphold racial supremacist philosophy and ideology. In other words, the combined images of the real-life strong Black woman and the magical Negro open the way for the Negro spiritual woman as a genre image of a controlled type of Black women's heroism that does not translate into the real world, and that justifies the current treatment of her, inadvertently exposing the genre's and society's racial biases.

From the inception of this country and before, images of oversexed Black women have permeated our conscientiousness. These are most apparent in films, literature, and other popular media. In the seminal film *Birth of a Nation* (1915), a blackface maid flutters on stage,[3] swinging saucy hips, while attempting to manipulate white men into sexual relations with her. Since that time, this image of the highly sexualized Black woman has not diminished. Also, both on and off the screen, Black women are often categorized as strong and fiercely independent, in the image of the strong Black woman. This archetype describes a Black woman who is unusually strong in comparison to her white female counterparts and sacrifices her own happiness for others—whether they are her children, the community, or her white employers. Within the speculative genre, the image of the magical Negro has evolved as a type of silent hero that is mostly Black and male. However, for Black women in the genre, these two images have evolved into a seemingly powerful representation of strong, self-assured authority: the Negro spiritual woman.

The real-life stereotype of the strong Black woman is depicted as a woman who willingly and quietly suffers without help, supporting others selflessly and without reward to herself. In *Behind the Mask of the Strong Black Woman*, Tamara Beauboeuf-Lafontant explains that a "discourse of strength is deployed to render Black women into self-disciplining bodies who uphold the social order" (Beauboeuf-Lafontant 36). Supposedly a positive image, this stereotype is constructed as an example of true Black womanhood. The strong Black woman does not complain about her place in society and is held up as an example of how others should be. She is content, accepting, and although not necessarily happy, she is proud of the society she supports.

Likewise, although created purely through fictional media, the magical Negro serves a similar purpose to the strong Black woman stereotype. Matthew Hughey elaborates in his article "Cinethetic Racism: White Redemption and Black Stereotypes in 'Magical Negro' Films":

> The MN has become a stock character that often appears as a lower class, uneducated Black person who possesses supernatural or magical powers. These powers are used to save and transform disheveled, uncultured, lost, or broken whites (almost exclusively white men) into competent, successful, and content people within the context of the American myth of redemption and salvation. (Hughey 544)

The strong Black woman, like the magical Negro, suffers quietly, without condemning the society that has oppressed her. The character is supportive of whites, does not normally have a family of her own, and is seemingly empowered. Likewise, within the genre, the Negro spiritual woman supports white society and is usually depicted as sexually provocative, almost solely for the benefit of white males.

Several recent blockbuster genre movies show that endowment of supernatural powers to Black women characters often does not bestow real power to Black women, and instead does the opposite by only offering them just enough authority to maintain the current societal structure, so as not to upset the racial and gender hierarchy within the films or society. The mystical powers granted to Black women by these films, as written by white creators, are quite possibly *anti-hero* powers, as they are in fact meant to offer Black women superheroes no hope or freedom from an oppressive society. This chapter will contextualize the trope of the Negro spiritual woman as it relates to popular Black women characters in modern films. These characters are chosen specifically, not only because they are popular, but because they have been well received as positive images of Black women.

The first notable example of the Negro spiritual woman genre image is Tia Dalma, from two of the popular *Pirates of the Caribbean* films. Introduced as Davy Jones's[4] ex-lover, Dalma is a flirty seductress who is more than willing to help the white characters for little or no reward. Originally the powerful goddess Calypso,[5] she once held control over the seas and everything within. Now she is "bound" into human form because she rejected

Pirates of the Caribbean: At World's End (2006). Giant Tia Dalma turning into crabs (Verbinski).

her white male lover, Davy Jones, and her power is reduced to only aiding the heroes on their journey, as she has been denied one of her own.

Dalma's character, within the Pirates of the Caribbean films *Dead Man's Chest* (2006) and *At World's End* (2007), is focused on sexual innuendos and resurrecting several of the dead white male characters. We are first introduced to Dalma when Captain Jack Sparrow, the hero, tells his men not to worry or to be afraid of the Black woman as the two of them "go way back" (*Dead Man's Chest*). After greeting Sparrow seductively—"Jack Sparrow. I always done known the wind would blow you back to me one day"—Dalma sets about flirting with another young white male character, Will Turner, advising him that he "holds a touch of destiny" (*Dead Man's Chest*). Although Dalma has been cursed and bound into human form by white men, it seems she cannot resist using her mystical powers to help them secure their fates as she immediately gives the group the information they need through her special ability to read crab claws.[6] When the crew returns after Jack has fallen to the Kraken, Dalma, having predicted his demise, produces a resurrected Barbossa (another white male captain) to save Jack Sparrow. Though Dalma has perfected the ability to resurrect the dead, she cannot resurrect herself so easily. We soon learn that Dalma brings both men back to life to free herself from her current form, but it is a complicated process that requires "pieces of eight," the talismans carried by both Sparrow and Barbossa. It's important to note that although it seems relatively easy for white men to reclaim their past lives as if they are deserved, it is intrinsically more difficult for the Black female character. She must bargain, accepting the value of white male life, before she can value her own. It is as if the world and, by extent, life itself belong to white men. More powerful Black female beings, such as Tia Dalma, must work harder to prove they are deserving.

Dalma vows that when she is returned to her natural form "the last thing [that Sparrow and Barbossa] will learn in life is how cruel [she] can be," and she offers to "give [Davy Jones] her heart" again (*At World's End*). However, when Calypso is free, she discovers that Davy Jones is responsible for enslaving her to human form.[7] Angry, Calypso grows to sixty feet tall, collapses into thousands of crabs which escape into the sea, and causes a giant storm that overtakes the ships. In the end, the newly returned Calypso does not take her revenge on the two characters that she has vowed to punish. Instead, the white male protagonist, Jack Sparrow, is left to continue his journey, as the Black woman returns quietly to the sea. The message is clear. Black women are meant to support white men. If they are unwilling to do this, the punishment is swift and uncompromising. Dalma is, however temporarily, relegated to a mere shadow of her former self until she is thoroughly contained, and society is better for it. Without Dalma's submissiveness, the journey of the white men would be in jeopardy and society would be threatened by her Black superpowers. Instead, she is depicted as an overly strong, sexual woman who is regulated to a submissive role for the benefit of this wider fictionalized world.

Looking at another well-known image of a Black woman within genre films, Kee from *Children of Men* (2006) comes readily to mind. Based on the novel of the same name, *Children of Men* is about a futuristic society where women have stopped being able to bear children. The world's youngest child has just been murdered, and societies across the globe are distraught and in ruin "because really, since women [have] stopped being able to have babies, [there's nothing] left to hope for" (*Children of Men*). The main character, Theo, is tasked with taking care of seemingly the last pregnant woman on earth. The woman, Kee, a West African refugee to the United Kingdom, is on the run because many people are after her and her unborn child.

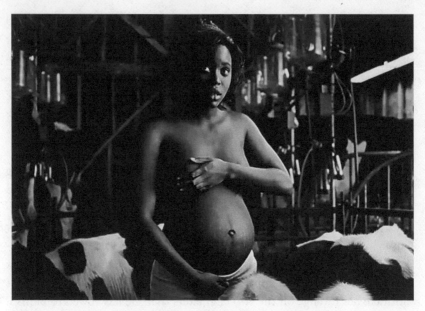

Children of Men (2006). Kee exposing her naked body to Theo (Cuarón).

Kee reveals her pregnancy to Theo by completely disrobing and showing her naked body. In a barn full of cows and milking equipment belying the infertile world, Kee's dark skin and plump belly expose her otherness. Not only are immigrants, such as Kee, routinely rounded up and placed in concentration camps, but she is the only known fertile woman in the world. Standing naked in the stall, Kee is, like all of the other animals, simply another creature to be herded and milked for the contributions that her offspring will bring to the world. She has very little value on her own, other than the fact that she can reproduce. Her sexuality, as it is in many other controlling images of Black women, is constructed for the benefit of the movie, and by extension, society. Like a slave woman at auction, Kee exposes her body to the white male character so that he can take control of her. Unlike an enslaved person, however, Kee's character willingly gives herself over to Theo in exchange for his protection. Theo's whiteness acts as a shield for Kee within the movie, and through him she is able to move more freely as long as her pregnant body, and thus her sexuality, is not exposed.

This image is further complicated when the young woman is asked who the father of her child is, "Whiffet! I'm a virgin," she responds. And then, right away, revealing the joke: "Nah! Be great, though, wouldn't it? Fuck knows. I don't know half the wankers' names. You know, when I started fucking, thought I'd catch the pest, but my belly started getting big" (*Children of Men*). The joke here is not that the idea of a virgin is archaic or outdated in 2027 society (there is much Christian symbolism within the film[8]), but seemingly that the idea that a Black woman could ever represent the virgin is itself absurd. Instead Kee is pictured, as society has portrayed Black women since well before the advent of film, as a confluence of strong Black woman and jezebel, a sexually aggressive deviant who does not care about herself or her child. It is revealed that Kee has had sex with many men without thought to her future or her body. This is reinforced in the end when Theo issues Kee a stern warning before he dies, having sacrificed himself for the mother and child. "Keep her close, Kee," the man says, "keep her close" (*Children of Men*). Theo's advice for her to take care of her daughter is cemented in the idea that Black women, and by extension, Kee, cannot be good mothers.[9] As far as the audience is concerned Theo is probably correct in warning Kee, as her character has been all but infantilized and constructed through the negative image of Black motherhood, and the audience is left unsure of her ability to take care of her own child.

It would be easy to argue that because Kee does not have supernatural powers she can't be contained by them; but Kee, more than any of the other characters in *Children of Men*, is directly subjugated through her sexuality and, more specifically, the power of her womb. Kee's power, like Mary's in the Christian Bible, comes from being the mother of the new, burgeoning world. Unlike Mary, however, Kee is constructed as a hyper-sexed vixen that is incapable of mothering. Instead, as the film ends, she is waiting to be taken into custody by government forces, so that she is—rightfully, in the world of the story—controlled. Considering that Kee is always in the control of whites within the film, it's easy to see that her unique power to bear children does not protect her, but instead contains her.

For Kee, being gifted with the ability to bear the last child on earth is not enough to change her position in life. In fact, this ability is oppressive for her, as it compounds the racism she already receives as a Black woman in futuristic, apartheid Britain. As a Black woman in the racist, dying society, Kee is oppressed, with very little hope of overcoming this position. However, by the end of the movie, viewers are contented, as she has been contained and put safely away from the society at large. In the end, viewers can ignore her position. They can feel comfortable in the idea that her powers bring her no real freedom from even this fictional, oppressive society.

One final example that cannot be overlooked is Hushpuppy from *Beasts of the Southern Wild* (2012). The movie is magical realism about a six-year-old Black girl, Hushpuppy, who lives in the southern Louisiana bayou in a community called the "Bathtub." The little girl lives with her father, who disappears for days at a time, leaving Hushpuppy to fend for herself. Her father eventually returns wearing a hospital gown and arm band and acting confused. Meanwhile, in school, Hushpuppy and the other children in the community are taught about the melted ice caps, which, they are told, released prehistoric creatures called "Aurochs." Hushpuppy conflates the levees breaking during hurricane Katrina to the release of the Aurochs, which she imagines chasing her throughout the film. As her father lies dying, Hushpuppy eventually confronts the Aurochs that have been causing her and her community distress, while the people watch and support her. In the end, the giant beasts nod their acceptance and leave Hushpuppy and her community to bury her dead father.

Hushpuppy is a tough character, often taking care of herself (despite her age) for days at a time, due to her missing, ill father, and there is no question that she is the embodiment of the strong Black woman stereotype. In her article "No Love in the Wild," bell hooks says, "Hushpuppy has a resilient spirit. She is indeed a miniature version of the 'strong black female matriarch' [that] racist and sexist representations have depicted from slavery on into the present day" (hooks). At one point during the film, the six-year-old punches her father for slapping her and causes him to pass out, as if due to her strength alone. The message, of course, is that Hushpuppy is capable of taking care of herself and so the audience need not sympathize too much with her. Although her father is abusive, and a six-year-old is not normally expected to defend herself from an adult who has attacked her, this is expected of Hushpuppy. Her Black skin is not obviously damaged from the attack, and she is "resilient." Because Hushpuppy is strong on her own, the viewers are content in the knowledge that she does not need their help—as, for instance, a young white girl in this position would—because she is fully capable of doing it herself. Strong Black women always are. Instead, the girl is charged with taking care of the community and "mothering" them, as she protects them from the savage beast plaguing the broken town. Since Hushpuppy is expected to mother instead of be mothered, in the end, when her father dies, the audience does not question how the young girl will survive. We are instead secure in the understanding that she is going to endure the trials of her future life if not completely overcome them, as is usually desired for white characters in her position.

Although Hushpuppy is, as bell hooks says, eroticized as a child, "[in] all manner of dirt and filth," she is not completely sexualized (hooks, "No Love"), as previously discussed characters have been. She wears baggy clothes, including a loose tee shirt and shapeless boy briefs. In this way, Hushpuppy is, unmistakably, a child—though she is a particularly mature one. At one point in the film, Hushpuppy goes to a brothel to find her mother. Although the male patrons are present as the women of the brothel "mother" Hushpuppy and her friends, it is clear that the young girl does not belong in this place. When the woman Hushpuppy has chosen as her mother holds her in her arms, the girl whispers: "I can count on two hands the times when I've been lifted up" (*Beasts*). As any young girl of her age would, Hushpuppy does not notice the sexual availability of scantily clad women, and simply seeks out the one that she can call mother.

Unfortunately, however, although the film does not completely sexualize her, the public reacted differently, as if to correct what they saw as the Black child moving outside of her constructed space or being too "uppity."

Quvenzhané Wallis, the nine-year-old actress who plays Hushpuppy, arrived at the 2013 Oscars showing her "guns"[10] to mimic the character in the movie, a smile splashed across her face. Obviously, this offense of being

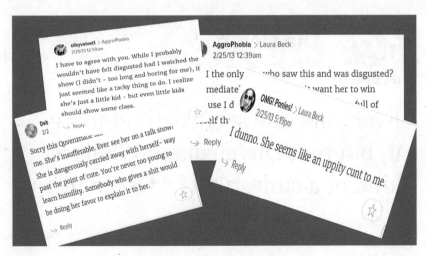

Only a small sample of comments by anti-Black genre fans.

"full of herself" is not to be forgiven. When the feminist weblog Jezebel posted an image of the girl, the comments exploded in response. They include: "Am I the only one who saw this [little girl] and was disgusted? I immediately decided I didn't want her to win because I don't want her to get any more full of herself than she seemed right there"; "it just seemed like a tacky thing to do. I realize she's just a little kid—but even little kids should show some class"; and "Sorry this Quvenzhané kid annoys the fuck outta me. She's insufferable. Ever see her on a talk show? She is dangerously carried away with herself— way past the point of cute. You're never too young to learn humility. Somebody who gives a shit would be doing her a favor to explain it to her" (Beck). Many replies rightly suggest that this strong reaction has everything to do with race, as young white actresses such as Dakota Fanning or Emma Watson never received such hatred. Young Ms. Wallis is simply "insufferable" because her Black skin[11] does not inspire adoration and thus she is perceived to be stepping outside of her designated submissive role. In fact, the message for the young Black actress seems clear: she is too uppity and needs to behave more like white America's idea of what a "good" Black girl should.

Because the audience cannot reconcile the cute little humble Black child of their imaginations with the confident, willful one that they see before them, they begin to objectify her, placing her within a more stereotypical, sexualized role that they are more familiar with.

During the same awards show, host Seth McFarlane cracked a joke at the actress's expense: "So let me just address those of you up for an award. So,

The Onion
@TheOnion

Everyone else seems afraid to say it, but that Quvenzhané Wallis is kind of a cunt, right? #Oscars2013

2/24/13, 11:42 PM

The Onion.

you got nominated for an Oscar, something a nine-year-old could do! She's adorable, Quvenzhané. She said to me backstage. 'I really hope I don't lose to that old lady, Jennifer Lawrence.' To give you an idea how young she is, it'll be sixteen years before she's too old for Clooney." Another joke aimed at Wallis is from the satirical site, The Onion, which tweeted, "Everyone else seems afraid to say it, but that Quvenzhané Wallis is kind of a cunt, right?" Both of these "jokes" center on the nine-year-old actress's sexuality. Not only does McFarlane suggest that it is not a big deal to be nominated for an Oscar, because, well, even this nine-year-old Black girl could do it, but he directs the audience to picture her as sexually available for older white men. The Onion tweet, of course, is more direct. It outright states that Wallis is nothing more than her female genital parts, as if to say, like those commenting on Jezebel, that the Black girl has moved outside of where The Onion believes she should be. This term is meant, unmistakably, to not only put Wallis in her place, but to ensure that she does not have movement outside of where the white populace imagines her. There is nothing in the movie to suggest that Wallis is either sexually available for men old enough to be her grandfather, or a "cunt." Unlike other Black women in the genre, Hushpuppy is not sexualized on-screen, although she is the representation of the strong Black woman and the magical Negro, as she is the only one with the power to exorcise the Aurochs. But this is not enough for society. They seem to need to contain Wallis as the other images of Black women in the genre have been contained. For this reason, the public sexualizes Quvenzhané Wallis themselves, as if they are adding to the script what is missing: the domination and sexual humiliation of this young Black woman.

Despite the difficulty for Black women in the genre, they have long worked to combat the negative images of themselves. Radford-Hill explains why this is important:

> Black women must develop identities that will not destroy them, but the broader society does not give us much with which to work. For example, history hands us identities built on racist stereotypes like mammy, auntie, prissy, jezebel, sapphire, bitch, video ho, and welfare queen. The social movements of the 1960s and 1970s handed us identities that appeared radical but required an odd combination of activism against racism and submission to sexism. (1085)

For Black women to be fully represented, they have begun to form their own identities within a genre that has shown itself to be hostile toward their presence. Notable Black women film directors are Kasi Lemmons, director of *Eve's Bayou* (1997) and Julie Dash, director of *Daughters of the Dust* (1991). Each of these movies have Black women protagonists and can easily be placed in the genre category. A more recent example of community support within the genre is with the 2014 short film *Danger Word*, by Black woman writer Tananarive Due and her husband, Steven Barnes. Fully funded through crowd sharing, the film raised nearly $15,000, surpassing their original $12,500 goal. The film is directed by Black woman director Luchlna Fisher and follows a thirteen-year-old Black girl, Kendra Brookings, and her grandfather during a zombie apocalypse. Unlike the previously described characters, Kendra does not accept the abuse of white society, putting aside their needs, and she finds strength within her family, particularly her grandfather, who does not sexualize her. Although empowered, Kendra is not simply a strong Black woman nor a magical Negro, and she is not endowed with superpowers that do not offer her hope. When Kendra's grandfather is bitten by a zombie, she must use the sharpshooting skills that he has taught her to save herself and secure her future. Kendra is not submissive, mysterious, nor overly sexual. For Kendra, and many of the other characters directed by Black women, society does not offer protection; instead, they choose to protect themselves, subverting the status quo. Because of this Kendra, as a Black female genre protagonist, does not have anti-heroic powers, but instead actually crosses over into full heroism.

Powerfully created supernatural characters, such as heroes in genre movies, often either live in a society that has created them or is of their own culture, so they fight for a society that supports and accepts them. These powerful characters uphold the oppressive laws because they are mutually beneficial for the society and for the heroes themselves. But for Black women who are often alienated within the society, the speculative genre creates a world not so different from ours, in which the Negro spiritual woman has no option other than to uphold the status quo. However, as Morrison states about the absence of the Black presence in society; the lack of Black women within the genre is central to our understanding of the hierarchy within that genre (5). Likewise, the Negro spiritual woman is created simply to fit into the world of the white creator, despite the appearance of acceptance within the genre. Instead, these genre conventions very well may create a space where Black women are more subjected through the bestowment of supernatural powers, as that appearance leaves the mostly white audience unthreatened in their patriarchal and racial positions in society. Ultimately, however, the most detrimental facet of this problem is not that there are negative images of Black women within the genre, but that instead there are rarely any positive contrasting images to combat the hurtful ones.

So where does this leave Storm, one of the most powerful beings in all the superhero universe? Up until this point, we have mostly discussed films in relation to the Negro spiritual woman stereotype, but what about the original comic book character, Storm? Has the relatively unrestricted freedom that comics offer likewise offered freedom from the constraints of white supremacy for this Black woman character?

Or has she, as Audre Lorde suggests, been "eaten alive" by white supremacists' fantasy of her (129)?

3

The "Funnies" as a Discipline

•••••••••••••••••••••

In grad school at Georgia State University while pursuing my degree in African American Studies, I had a professor who loved to call my research on comics "playing with the funnies." We both laughed, as it was harmless, good-natured ribbing. She was an older Black woman who researched serious subjects like the Mau Mau Rebellion in Kenya and Kikuyu women, and she grew up in an era when the "funnies" were comic strips in newspapers which featured weird, white people who went on strange adventures. The funnies were for white people and about white people. But like everything else, the absence of Black people in the *Sunday Funnies* and other magazines shows us that the lack of representation of racial diversity is indicative of the function of our society. My professor knew this. At her retirement party, I told her I wanted to be like her, and she hugged me and whispered that I could be much bigger, aim higher, and have the potential to reach and inspire more people.

This book is an attempt to make the funnies a "serious" subject, critiquing the way images and controlling stereotypes impact us all, but particularly Black women and girls.

This chapter discusses why it is important to look at comics as more than just the funnies. The chapter is broken into two sections on history and

The Funnies Issue 24 (1938). Comics.org.

theory. The first looks at the history behind stereotypes and the second examines the theory behind the creation of the Black woman superhero. While theory and history are not necessarily fun topics, if we don't examine history and apply theory, we cannot fully understand our present and correct problems in the future. But also, although I am a fiction writer by heart, any academic writing must have a sound foundation from which to start. This my foundation.

History and Why It's Important to Understand Stereotypes

Stereotypes work because they seem to outline realistic images of the groups that they represent. For example, according to research presented at the British Science Festival in Aberdeen in 2012, stereotypes evolve in a "similar way to language," so as to be able to make sense of complicated ideas around certain groups. It should also be argued that stereotypes work to find an outlet for xenophobia in the public sphere.

While defining and researching traditional stereotypes in film is important, it's equally important to realize that within genre fiction such as comics, these traditional images are not stationary. Stereotypes themselves are not static. They change and evolve to continue to function within a society that needs to contain certain groups and bodies.

For instance, in his autobiography published in 1845, *Narrative of the Life of Frederick Douglass, an American Slave, and Written by Himself*, the author criticizes the stereotype of the happy slave, singing as they work for the delight of their masters.

During this same time, freed Black people were conceptualized as more prone to disease. Terms such as "drapetomania" were coined to argued that a disease caused Black people to resist enslavement. In May 1851, Dr. Samuel A. Cartwright published his article in the *New Orleans Medical and Surgical Journal*, which read:

> Drapetomania is from draptise. A runaway slave is mania mad or crazy. It is unknown to our medical authorities, although its diagnostic symptoms be absconding from service, is well known to our planters and overseers. In noticing a disease that, therefore, is hitherto classed among the long list of maladies that man is subject to, it was necessary to have a new term to express

it. The cause in most cases that induces the Negro to run away from service is as much a disease of the mind as any other species of mental alienation, and much more curable as a general rule. With the advantages of proper medical advice strictly followed, this troublesome practice that many Negroes have of running away can be almost entirely prevented, although the slaves are located on the borders of a free state within a stone's throw of abolitionists. (691)

The anger that Douglass expresses in his writing is from the revelation that those with power often use it to create harmful stereotypes against those without power—and due particularly to that power, those stereotypes become the narrative around which subordinate groups must navigate. The harmful construction of the happy enslaved Black person who willingly suffers for the benefit of white people was created simply to justify chattel slavery. This stereotype functions to do nothing other than uphold slavocracy and white dominance over Black bodies, positioning Black people as willingly complicit in their own subjugation. The argument is that if Black people are happy to be enslaved, then there is no reason to eliminate slavery; it rationalizes their enslavement. Images of content, enslaved Black people permeated all facets of American life and seeped well into the twentieth century and beyond. The 1939 film *Gone with the Wind* is just one example. An image search for the title *A Birthday Cake for George Washington*, which is about one of Washington's slaves who excitedly works to bake him a birthday cake (Ramin and Brantley-Newton), serves as evidence that this stereotype is an active part of our construction of Black people to this day.

Once Black people openly resisted and revolted against their enslavement,[1] however, the stereotype changed. Post Nat Turner (1831) and other slave rebellions, white Americans claimed that Black Americans[2] needed to be enslaved and strictly controlled because they were too vicious to be free, and thus the stereotype of the violent, murderous, Black brute was shaped. The stereotype at that point was of violent Black hordes killing white people. The black and white image here clearly (figure 12) depicts Black men slaughtering white women, men and children, as white men ride in to protect white people from harm. Absent from the picture, of course, is the brutality of chattel slavery and the conditions that brought Black people to the point of resistance in the first place. In this case, the reality of chattel slavery would disrupt the stereotype of a Black threat against white people, so it needed to be avoided.

A Birthday Cake for George Washington by Ramin Ganeshram and Vanessa Brantley-Newton (2016). Indoctrination of children through the happy, content slave image.

Horrid Massacre in Virginia. Library of Congress.

It's important to recognize that stereotypes are not "truth" as usually described, but instead they represent the narrative created and continuously recreated to maintain whatever image and ideology is needed at that time. Stereotypes often function for the benefit of the mainstream society, and rarely advantage minority groups.

Stereotypes are the perfect mechanism for oppression.

More relevant for the purposes of this book are the varying stereotypes of Black women which effectively work to oppress us. Moving back briefly to Patricia Hill Collins, controlling images (a kind of stereotype) function in society to maintain the status quo (77). They have existed since well before the advent of slavery and change and evolve as the society needs to maintain or gain more control over Black and minority peoples. Collins states that controlling images serve several functions: They help to normalize oppression by making it appear that the oppressed person is happy or content, or that they need to be controlled because it is in the oppressed person's best interests; and controlling images serve to intimidate oppressed groups into their own oppression while ensuring that oppressors feel the need to oppress to maintain order (P. H. Collins 77–79).

Collins identifies four central controlling images for Black women, which are the mammy, the matriarch, the welfare mother, and the jezebel. She states that "the dominant ideology of the slave era fostered the creation of four interrelated, socially constructed controlling images of Black womanhood, each reflecting the dominant group's interest in maintaining Black women's subordination" (P. H. Collins 76). These images are not only used to oppress Black women, but to make this oppression appear normal and even necessary. Likewise, Collins suggest that controlling images do not reflect the true reality of Black women, but instead categorizes them within these limited spaces. While Collins identifies four of these images, to be brief, only three are outlined here, as they will be necessary later: the mammy, matriarch, and jezebel.

Summing up the scholarship collected in *The Kaleidoscope of Gender*, Joan Spade and Catherine Valentine state that "variations in gender (and racial) stereotypes act as controlling images that maintain complex systems of domination and subordination in which some individuals and groups are dehumanized and disadvantaged in relationship to others" (xv). Other research suggests that "stereotypes represent externally-defined, controlling images of Afro-American womanhood that have been central to the dehumanization of Black women and the exploitation of Black women's labor" (Fonow 38). Controlling images are specific images of racial minorities that seek to exploit and control members of those groups.

One of the most popular controlling images is that of the mammy. The image of the mammy has been imprinted on the U.S. consciousness since before the debut of the seminal film *Birth of a Nation* and continues to exist in popular culture today. P. H. Collins states:

> The first controlling image applied to U.S. Black women is that of the mammy—the faithful, obedient domestic servant. Created to justify the economic exploitation of house slaves and sustained to explain Black women's long-standing restriction to domestic service, the mammy image represents the normative yardstick used to evaluate all Black women's behavior. By loving, nurturing, and caring for her White children and "family" better than her own, the mammy symbolizes the dominant group's perceptions of the ideal Black female relationship to elite White male power. Even though she may be well loved and may wield considerable authority in her White "family," the mammy still knows her "place" as obedient servant. She had accepted her subordination. (80)

As a general rule, mammies are meant to be positive reflections of Black women, who are seen as caring and loving asexual individuals who adore and care for whites to the exclusion of themselves and the Black community. Other research adds that this archetype is not meant "to reflect or represent a reality but function as a disguise, or mystification, of objective social relations" (Carby 69). In other words, the objective of stereotypes is not only to make race, class, and gender biases acceptable, but to make them necessary for the society to function as it does.

Such is the case of the mammy. P. H. Collins states that this submissive character further "supports racial superiority" while allowing whites to feel comfortable in their positions of power (80). Through this white racial alliance, the mammy caricature does not threaten white authority and further allows for the manipulation of the Black presence and positioning of Black women through these fictions.

A single image alone, of course, is not enough to control Black women. Other images are constantly evolving, and being created to replace older stereotypes, "explaining Black women's placement in intersecting oppressions" (P. H. Collins 82). Brown states that there are "myriad ways the black female body has been othered, functioning simultaneously as an anathema and an enigma with U.S. society" and "have been consistently misnamed, misconstrued, and rendered as scapegoats" (68). Likewise, scholars have indicated that Black women "have endured a long history of interlocking oppressions at the intersection of sexism, racism and classism" (Windsor et al. 291).

The controlling image of the jezebel, researchers say, "is a biblical figure portrayed in the Books of Kings as a conniving harlot devoted to false Gods" and that the image was "imposed on dark-skinned native women by puritan European men" in order to justify their oppression and rape (Windsor et al. 291). The jezebel fosters the idea that Black women are sexually "insatiable" and promiscuous and thus "cannot be raped because they enjoy sex under any circumstance" (Windsor et al. 292). This image is important to recognize because, as researchers suggest, "efforts to control Black women's sexuality lie at the heart of Black women's oppression, [and] historically jezebels . . . represent a deviant Black female sexuality" (P. H. Collins 89). Unlike the mammy, who is often asexual, the jezebel is sexually assertive and dominant and thus must be controlled to stem her "deviant" sexual desires (P. H. Collins 92).

Gilkes states that "Black women emerged from slavery firmly enshrined in the consciousness of white America as 'Mammy' and the 'bad black woman'" (294). Another example of the bad Black woman lies in the image of the matriarch: "[The] Black matriarch fulfills similar functions in explaining Black women's placement in intersecting oppressions" (P. H. Collins 82). Further, "while the mammy typifies the Black mother figure in White homes, the matriarch symbolizes the mother figure in Black homes. As the mammy represents the 'good' Black mother because she is willing to unconditionally submit to whiteness, the matriarch symbolizes the 'bad' Black mother" because she controls her own sexuality (P. H. Collins 83). This image is used to control Black women, suggesting that they spend too much time away from her own children working to support their families, emasculate Black men, and are aggressive and unloving to their families. In other words, the matriarch represents the "failed mammy," with the mammy often seen as the only positive Black female figure (P. H. Collins 83). This image, as the ones before it, supports racial oppression.

The problem with controlling images, of course, is that "living in a segregated society, white Americans learn about African Americans not through personal relationships but through the images the media show them" (Entman and Rojecki 206). When Black people are expected to fulfill the expectations of stereotypes that whites have created, they are not offered autonomy within the broader society. This not only limits their mobility and keeps Black people stagnant in society, but it reaffirms the negative stereotypes already in force in the media.

In a study in 2005, researchers suggest that while Black actors are now more numerous in film and literature, their images are rarely positive, and they are still wholly underrepresented in proportion to their white counterparts (Entman and Rojecki 11).

The research further suggests that, like African American men, mediated portrayals of African American women influence judgments of those same African American women in social situations (Glenn and Cunningham 136). The researchers found that research participants were quicker to associate African American women with negative terms such as "aggressive" than with positive terms such as "sincere." They also found that participants who had encountered controlling images prior to the study related African American women to those stereotypes, such as the mammy. Researchers observed that the familiar mammy role assigned to Black women has a negative effect on the way Black women, both historically and in present day, view themselves. Furthermore, the research found that the mammy role has now been expanded into corporate America and includes Black female clerical, managerial, specialty-type technical, business, and professional employees. These studies are useful in that they address the concept of controlling images and offer evidence that we continue to maintain these stereotypes within society (Abdullah 134).

While stereotypes are a mainstay in our society, and sociological and other research has worked to show both the necessary and detrimental aspects of stereotypes, little if any research has touched on the way these stereotypes function when dealing with characters who are not considered "real." This offers several challenges to answer in this book. First and foremost is the idea that superheroes are not only created, but that they, like cartoons or commercials, are not meant to be taken seriously and thus should not be considered worthy of critique.

Luckily, more and more recent scholarship has helped to combat this idea, though it persists in some ways. In addition, this research argues that not only is it important to understand and define stereotypes to understand them, but that superheroes and characters with superhuman powers work quite differently than non-supernatural characters in society, and it is important to redefine stereotypes as we know them to understand the full breadth of the way these harmful images permeate our consciousness. We need to constantly examine the construction of new and old stereotypes to analyze how they evolve within our society, even as they pertain to "fake" people, such as Storm or Tara Thornton. Many existing stereotypes, such as the magical Negro, represent these types of characters as they function now. However, it has become important to identify other, more appropriate ones for these supernaturally gifted characters.

To address the argument that comic books and cartoons, should not be taken seriously, readers might ask themselves how they developed their idea of what a hero is and how one behaves. While we can all name people from our own lives that represent our personal ideas of who a hero should be, we cannot discount the power that well-established figures such as Captain America have within society. In other words, while your father is a hero to you, Superman, for instance, has been the hero to seven decades of people. Those two do not compare. As such, it is important to examine speculative media just as critically as we do all other forms of art and literature—and society.

Science fiction and fantasy author Samuel R. Delany brought this point home for me. He once explained to me that after the troops were slowly integrated in World War II, war movies began to allow solitary Black characters into war films to portray this perceived integration.[3] As a result, genre writer Robert Heinlein "took this strategy" for his books which "knocked reader's socks off" because it had not been done before in literature.[4] Delany went on to explain that this strategy ensured that there are often never two or more Black characters on the screen together for fear that they will sneak off and team up to plan a takeover or revolution of their own. Instead, Delany suggests, this implies that the Black characters within these stories are supposed to be content in their position subservient to whites; to show plurality is to unwillingly highlight possible disruption in an otherwise content society that was not ready to deal with true integration. The point here, of course, is that even within fiction and fantasy worlds, ideologies and stereotypes are used to uphold racial injustice.

Although by some definitions this segregation of Black characters has changed, examining current media (movies, literature, and so on) suggests that old stereotypes have not been eliminated as much as they have simply evolved slightly. Because of this, movies become a type of substitute for information on race, class, and gender issues when people have no other frame of reference from which to pull. Glenn and Cunningham state:

> Millions of people flock to theaters to view the fantasy world that Hollywood has created, all the while processing a large amount of information that guides their formation and expectations in actual society. The projected images pertaining to the interaction and relationship between people from different ethnic and racial backgrounds have significant implications for audience members' perceptions of race relations. (135)

In other words, movies affect stereotypes and the negative images that people have of minority peoples. Whites who have had little to no interaction with Black people will likely form their opinions of them through the media that they consume. In the same vein, researchers found that other media forms, such as TV news, are two times more likely to show mugshots of criminal defendants if they are Black rather than white (Entman and Rojecki 168). Additionally, this research suggests that television advertisements now show many Black people in stereotypical roles, more often than not in supportive roles to whites, and not the other way around. Unsurprisingly, Kellner states that "media images help shape our view of the world and our deepest values: what we consider good or bad, positive or negative, moral or evil" (Dines and Humez 5).

It is no wonder, then, that Glenn and Cunningham suggest that whites that have no contact with Black people think they know about them because of scripted roles for Blacks written by mostly white authors (136). The media plays a role in disseminating this scripted information to the public, and the public in turn feels that they have gained a firsthand account of the lives of Black people, without having to interact with Black men and women in the real world. In this case, the media becomes the creator of a fictional idea of Blackness, and the public becomes experts of a fictional Black identity. Black people function only as entertainment to whites and, more importantly, they are often depicted solely as subservient or to feed the fears of a mainly white audience.

In relation to comic books, Jennifer Ryan explains that "narratives rely on the tension between image and text" and this tension has been captured in many "classic works of American literature" (Ryan 922). Furthermore, Derek Royal explains that because comics are a "hybrid medium where image and text often breed an ambiguous yet pliable synthesis" they can be used to "challenge stereotypical representation of race and gender" (Royal 126). With that in mind, it can be argued that although comic books offer the possibility of highlighting this tension, they also provide the opportunity to simply reinforce racial and gender oppression.

To the point that it is important to define the stereotypes of characters with unimaginable powers in relation to their evolving stereotypes, we will look at the representation of Black women in the media. While it would be interesting to dismantle negative stereotypes of all Black people, this book will focus on Black women and comics specifically. More to the point, this analysis aligns with the *Combahee River Collective Statement*: "If Black women were free, it would mean that everyone else would have to be free since our freedom would necessitate the destruction of all the systems of oppression" (Combahee River Collective).

P. H. Collins states that "race, class and gender oppression could not continue without powerful ideological justifications for their existence" (66), and that "portraying African American women as stereotypical mammies, matriarchs, welfare recipients and hot mommas has been essential to political economy of domination fostering Black women's oppression" (67). Black women are underrepresented in the media, whether television or literature, and when we are shown, it is in overwhelmingly stereotypical depictions. This is also the case in works of literature and film, such as comic books.

Dorothy Roberts touches on this ideology as well. She states: "The social order established by powerful white men was founded on two inseparable ingredients: the dehumanization of Africans on the basis of race and the control of women's sexuality" (23). Here, it is important to acknowledge that society has always needed to control Black people, and that controlling Black women has become particularly paramount through their sexuality, including representation of Black women as mammies, who are generally asexual because their only concern is the whites for which they work. Likewise, in an interview in the *New York Times* in 1974, actress Ellen Holly is quoted as saying: "One of the penalties of being Black and having limited money is that we seldom control our own image. We seldom appear in media as who we say we are, but rather as who whites say we are" (Means Coleman 119). In other words, Black people, including Black women, have historically been misrepresented within white written works for the benefit of white audiences.

Toni Morrison argues that the "Africanist presence" is placed in fiction according to the needs and desires of its "white creator" and its presence has been there since the creation of the construct of race—or at least the beginning of the American slave trade (6). Most notably, though, she says that the Black presence is there even if it is ignored and especially if it is unrecognized. To put this in context, Blackness is a part of our social consciousness (in binary opposition to whiteness) and to ignore it exposes more about the society than about the people the society has alienated. This is no less true for the presence of Black women within our society. To that end, Black women within the genre are often absent, and that absence in itself is not only a statement about the genre as a whole but implies that the genre is invested in containing Black women in a similar fashion to the broader society. After all, comics empowering Black women, who are systemically oppressed through both their gender and race, would highlight that Black women are still very much oppressed within society.

Compared to the mammy character, the magical Negro is often considered a relatively new stereotype. Many scholars have tackled the image of the magical Negro. To reiterate, scholars say that the character is the "noble, good-hearted black man or woman" who is "saintly" and is "morally equal to their White counterparts" (Appiah 33). Researchers Entman and Rojecki outline three main purposes for the character: to assist the white character; to help the white character discover his/her own spirituality; and to offer folk wisdom for the white character's benefit (111).

Some researchers state that although scholars have discussed the character, the commentary seldom addresses how the magical Negro is a harmful, racist stereotype. They further assert that these "discussions overlook the images of women in these roles as well as dominant society's vested interest in fostering and maintaining oppressive controlling images for Black people" (Glen and Cunningham 139). Indeed, they believe, the image of the helpful servant role has its history in the classic controlling images of the mammy, jezebel, and Uncle Tom (138). It is important to note here that the magical Negro's power is only used to empower and protect whiteness and the needs of the white character. Having a white overseer for Black power contains both the Blackness and the power so that it is used for the benefit of the white status quo. Others explain it this way:

> Despite Black people' talents and abilities, they [are not thought to] know how to use [supernatural abilities] appropriately without someone to instruct them how to do so. The inversion of real-life power structure, the moral and spiritual superiority of Black characters, and the Whites' need to tap into this may also serve to alleviate White guilt with the current status Black people hold in actual society or to contribute to the belief that Black people possess the ability to change society with their gifts. This allows many Whites to hold the seeming contradictory belief that Black people have the ability to improve their social status, yet they do not have the ability to discern how to use their abilities. (Glenn and Cunningham 150)

Black people are kept contained within the character limitations of the magical Negro despite outward appearances that they are powerful and could affect social change if they choose to.

However, there is a more complicated relationship between the magical Negro and his white brethren, which echoes the society at large:

> When black actors are constantly cast as angels, spirits, Gods and other incarnate supernatural forces, they displace the realities of history into more viewer-friendly narratives. That is, the various filmmakers create scenes of trouble-free and uncomplicated black/white reconciliation. When racial,

social and cultural formations remain unmentioned and unquestioned, these reconciliation scenes are more effective. On the one hand, this basic narrative appeals to feelings among whites and Black people alike that there can be racial reconciliation and accord. . . . On the other hand, these films resonate with a racial crisis in the United States so unpleasant that it must be replaced by fantastical stories of magic. (Hughley 550)

I would be remiss not to address, also, that showing this false racial harmony serves to alleviate white guilt, allowing white people to ignore the racial inequality in a society in which whites participate and benefit. This allows whites not only to "displace realities of histories into [. . .] viewer friendly narratives" (Hughey 550), but also suggest that Black people who do not pre-form "friendliness" to white people are the true villains of white stories. If, likewise, Black people are content in these positions serving white people, which the magical Negro caricature suggests, then there is no reason to believe that racial inequality is anything but a thing of the past. Acknowledging that media impacts the way that people view the world suggests that whites may believe that this racial harmony is simply the way the world exists now and that any suggestion of inequality is race-baiting or only exists in the minds of nonconforming Black people. In this imaginary world, Black women effectively become the "good" Negro spiritual woman, or the "bad" angry Black woman, and there is little in between for our existence.

Theory behind Superheroes and the Creation of the Black Woman Superhero

To reiterate, comic books have a history in the United States dating back to the 1930s. The main characters in these books focus on superheroes or antiheroes who often possess superhuman powers and use those powers, whether willingly or reluctantly, to protect humanity. The stories often contain "genre" tropes such action, science fiction, fantasy, or horror elements.

Scholars state that "comic books are history" (Aiken 41). They often follow themes and plots in which the hero or heroes fight against an equally powerful antagonist to protect humanity. Katherine Aiken goes on to say that "as primary sources of popular culture, [comic books] have emerged from a specific context, reflecting the politics, prejudices, and concerns of a particular historical moment. Comics have also shaped the outlooks of America's young people" (41). We find examples of films based on this medium in motion pictures such as *Superman,* which first appeared in animated short films in 1941 and has repeatedly been adapted for the screen until its most recent incarnation as *Batman v Superman* (2016); *Spiderman,* which has had six films since its comic incarnation in 1962 (Duncan and Smith 28); and *Batman,* from which fans will remember animated action words such as "*KAPOW!*" in the 1960s television show that became a popular culture phenomenon. *Batman* ran on television from 1966 to 1968 and has been adapted in modern films starring George Clooney (*Batman and Robin,* 1997) and Christian Bale (*The Dark Knight Rises,* 2012).

While P. H. Collins and others have argued that the construction of stereotypes has always functioned to keep certain groups subordinate to the white populace, images of superheroes in popular culture have often distanced themselves from discussions of race and gender. Other researchers add that "although many scholars have addressed the manner in which young people construct their identities when engaging comic books, superheroes and heroic figures, race is rarely a central focus of such research because race is rarely an overt focus of comic books. Although this is not necessarily the intention of the screenwriters, it is folly to ignore the context provided by race" (Gayles 285). Gayles asserts that "black superheroes ... must bear the burden of race as an explanatory device," in the way that white superheroes often do not (285). It is, researchers suggest, an often-unspoken rule that these characters' Black bodies signify oppression despite, or perhaps directly because of, the inherent power boiling just underneath their dark skin.

For Black female superheroes, scholars write that "while black female superheroines may seem like they kick an awful lot of butt, a closer look reveals that their roles haven't changed much: For the most part, they're doomed to navigate the confines of poverty and war with infinite resolve or, failing that, risk descending into madness, drug abuse, or other social ills" (Saini 96). In this way, race and gender taken together are defining indicators of a character's position in the comic book world and the Black superhero characters are tasked with navigating these spaces, much as they are in real life.

Saini lists three dominant stereotypes that Black women inhabit within comic books. *The quiet queen* most often represents the image of the "Mother Earth" or "African Queen" and derives her power from "a closeness" with nature, is soft spoken, rises high in the ranks, but usually must "overcome adverse circumstances often associated with communities of color"; *the dominant diva* is the "archetype of the revolutionary black woman" and often chooses "emotional impulse over intellectual exploration"; and *the scandalous sojourner* is often the center of a cautionary tale about the evils of drug abuse and promiscuity" (Saini 96). With these in mind, Saini suggests that comic books are not free from the racist, sexist stereotypes that dominate the real world.

Scholars discuss the way the imagery of comic books plays on ideas of race:

> Comic books, and particularly the dominant genre of superhero comic books, have proven fertile ground for stereotyped depictions of race. Comics rely upon visually codified representations in which characters are continually reduced to their appearances, and this reductionism is especially prevalent in superhero comics, whose characters are wholly externalized into their heroic costumes and aliases. This system of visual typology combines with the superhero genre's long history of excluding, trivializing, or "tokenizing" minorities to create numerous minority superheroes who are marked purely for their race: "Black Lightning," "Black Panther," and so forth. The potential for superficiality and stereotyping here is dangerously high. (Singer, "Black Skins" 107)

Anna Beatrice Scott takes it a step further than Marc Singer, arguing that comic books move beyond simply being stereotypes into "tales that are informed by white supremacist visuality, circulating in mainstream culture as over-determined narration" (Scott 295).

> Discussing race and gender representations in comics, researchers found that "when analyzing [the] heroine behaviors [of the comic book character], it is clear that the depictions are largely gender and race stereotypical and thus detrimental to ... women in general, and ultimately other persons of color" (McGrath 281). Likewise, they suggest that although the X-Men comic books are considered one of the most "diverse franchises in the industry," upon examination the series is dominated by white male characters, and that although the series often condemns prejudice and discrimination, the actual heroic characters are most often white, with the threat coming from minority characters. (Darowski 3–4)

Because of their often-unexamined support of the white power structure, Black superheroes frequently walk a thin line between being superheroes that fight against injustice and magical Negroes who simply maintain allegiance to whites and use their powers in support of the status quo.

Researchers examine the fabric of the comic book era of the 1960s:

> Stan Lee and his shop of inkers and writers leapt into the fractured reality of the 1960s, seeking a market in a moment when tomorrow looked like a lie for sure. . . . And there stood the black bodies . . . looking like maps, saviors, madonnas and demons all at the same time. Supernatural. Adaptable, sturdy, jaded and still hopeful, the black bodied anti-citizens of the United States, suffering from that tragic magic as they did, instigated, demanded a new reality, one that ultimately could not be delivered (at least not evenly) by the subjects of white supremacy. (Scott 297)

Instead, comic books placed Black bodies in the place of white ones to express a false sense of racial equality, without having the characters challenge the status quo. This infusion of Blackness into the mostly white supernatural comic book world did two things: maintained the status quo and white domination over it; and often played on long held ideas of controlling images.

From the beginning, women comic superhero characters have always needed to walk a precarious line between being subversive and powerful and being the motherly figures that society expects from women: "there was undoubtedly, subversiveness in the superheroine. . . . However, the backbone of American conservatism during the latter half of the twentieth century was the nuclear family . . . and since there was only one nuclear family constructed in the mainstream superhero comic book universe between 1960–1980 . . . , comic books have to find other means of maintaining a recognizable social order with regard to gendering of roles" (D'Amore 1228). Furthermore, because comic books did not seek to subvert the social norms or the idea of the nuclear family, comic books had to find a way for the female comic hero to fall into line. D'Amore believes that how comic books accomplished this was through maternalizing the superheroine. "The superheroine," D'Amore maintains, "is a gendered body of contradiction, at once conservative and liberal, traditional and radical" (1228).

Wonder Woman is the most recognizable female superhero of all time. Second only to Superman and Batman, she is the longest-lasting comic book hero. Documenting the history of the characters, Lepore writes that "like every other superhero, she also has a secret history" (Lepore). Researchers explain that since the first issue of the comic book, people have been driven crazy in the search of Wonder Woman's identity and none have been able to find it. Wonder Woman is not only elusive, it seems, but for many she is a feminist icon. Lepore argues that "[t]he veil that has shrouded Wonder Woman's past for seven decades hides beneath it a crucial story about comic books and superheroes and censorship and feminism" (Lepore).

Wonder Woman first appeared in *All Star Comics*, issue number eight, in 1941. She is an Amazonian warrior princess, who is known as Princess Diana of Themyscira in her homeland. Her weapons include thick impenetrable bracelets, the Magic Lasso (Lasso of Truth), a tiara, and an invisible airplane. Wonder Woman is depicted fighting for justice, peace, and sexual equality. Her creator, William Marston, once stated, "Frankly, Wonder Woman is psychological propaganda for the new type of woman who, I believe, should rule the world" (Lepore).

Although Wonder Woman has always been in print, she found little success on the big screen until 2017, despite a short television appearance staring Lynda Carter that ran from 1975–1979. Since the television series ended, Wonder Woman struggled to find a motion-picture audience, despite being popular and featured in a variety of toys and merchandise, such as tee shirts and lunchboxes (Lepore, The Surprising Origin Story of Wonder Woman). The 2017 Wonder Woman film debuted to decent reviews, and the second one, in 2020, went straight to HBO Max but did not fare as well with reviewers.

Wonder Woman may finally be getting some recognition in films after a long history of being mostly ignored, however, it is relevant to examine her history within the world of superheroes when doing an analysis of Storm, because Wonder Woman is the preeminent female superhero. Julie O'Reilly writes:

> Although Wonder Woman, who debuted in *All-Star Comics* in 1941, challenged previous notions regarding the subordination of female superheroes to men, she was still not equal to her male counterparts. In Wonder Woman's first comic book story line, the Amazon princess Diana must compete in and win a series of physical challenges that culminate in a frightening and potentially deadly game of "bullets and bracelets" (i.e., deflecting gunshots with her wristbands) to prove to the Amazon

Queen—her mother—that she is a "Wonder Woman" worthy to venture into man's world to "fight for liberty and freedom and all womankind." In contrast, in the first Superman comic book story line published three years earlier, Clark Kent decides to don a cape and enforce justice—a decision that is neither questioned nor challenged. He becomes a hero simply because he chooses to be: "Early, Clark decided he must turn his titanic strength into channels that would benefit mankind. And so was created . . . Superman!" Thus, Wonder Woman's legacy is one of deference, or at the least, limited agency; Superman's is one of assumed autonomy. (O'Reilly 273)

O'Reilly explains that because of their respective genders, there are different levels of acceptance for each of these characters. For Wonder Woman this means that she must prove that she is worthy to protect the society from injustice, even when in many cases it is men who are creating these injustices. As such, female superheroes must be placed on "trial" before the public of comic book readers to prove that they are worthy, while males do not.

Likewise, Mitra Emad argues that Wonder Woman's body is the site of contradictions between both gender and nationality. The idea is that the human body is a cultural construction within U.S. society and that it functions as a site for cultural translations. Emad states:

[Wonder] Woman's body, often shown running, in star-spangled shorts in 1944 offers one style of imagined nationhood compared with a wide-eyed, large-breasted ingénue in 2001. In each historical instance, however, Wonder Woman's body is both an icon of the traditionally masculine, public realm of nationhood as well as the traditionally feminine, private realm of female sexuality. As such, her body serves as a site for constantly oppositional encounters between gender and nation, private and public, and bondage and power. Reading Wonder Woman's body is an exercise in swinging between the binaries of women's physical empowerment (and sexual freedom) and representations of a body in bondage, lassoed into submission, sometimes by her own power. (956)

Wonder Woman is an Amazon, not officially a U.S. citizen, and has to prove that she is capable of protecting the United States, but her body is adorned in the American flag and she must represent it above all other loyalties. As scholars suggest, this places Wonder Woman's national identity and gender in constant opposition to each other.

Not only are Wonder Woman's nationality and attire a site of contention, but so is her gender. Daniels believes that "Wonder Woman has always been obliged to play a dual role. In addition to keeping a large audience entertained with her exploits, she has also been expected to serve as a representative and an example for her entire gender, and the tension between these two responsibilities has given Wonder Woman a unique position in America's popular culture" (11). Wonder Woman, unlike other male superheroes before and after her, is expected to represent her entire gender. Black superheroes are expected to tackle race while others do not, and women superheroes are forced to represent and tackle gender dynamics. It is not a far leap, then, to understand that Black women superheroes sit on the cusp of representing both their gender and race.

Sexuality, although often hidden, is a reoccurring theme in comic books. Some scholars believe that "comic books have always revealed themes that can be identified as queer, as the majority of superheroes always had to live two lives, one as hero and one as civilian" (Peters 2). Peters further argues that "Wonder Woman encompasses the very pinnacle of queer themes, and since her inception into the world of DC comics she has exhibited varying degrees of both gay-drag and lesbian subtexts," and as a result, Wonder Woman has "served as a safe haven, a source of inspiration and a pre-liberation voice for many readers" (Peters 2). Here I want to highlight that marginalized groups find representation within the construction of Wonder Woman, suggesting more than anything that representation in media is not only impactful, but also gives voice to these groups.

Keeping in mind the discussion of controlling images and the efforts to control Black women's sexuality through these images, it is possible to surmise that Black women superheroes, such as Storm, are not offered the sexual freedom that their white female counterparts are given. Instead, as scholars suggest, Black female superheroes may be contained by their gender, race, and their superhuman powers do little to abate that subjugation.

While it is arguable that Wonder Woman offers a type of liberation to female and gay and queer readers through sexual freedom, Black female superheroes' sexual construction is colored by their identities as Black women in a white patriarchal society. Storm must navigate both that society and any Black community that seeks her protection.

Discussing the significance of how myth combined with the construction of race has affected popular culture and the genre specifically, Maurice Berger states:

Despite the visual sophistication and supposed vigilance of a media-oriented culture . . . Western commentators, critics, and academics seem not to realize how duplicitous words and images can be. They simply do not understand how myths work, how myths hold us hostage to their smooth elegant fictions. The subject of race, perhaps more than any other subject in contemporary life feeds on myth. . . . Myth is the book, seamless narrative that tells us the contradictions and incongruities of race and racism are too confusing or too dangerous to articulate. Myths provide the elegant deceptions that reinforce our unconscious prejudices. Myths are the white lies that tell us everything is all right, even when it is not. (92)

For comic books, the myths that Berger addresses are often predicated on the idea that race and gender issues are not important to a functioning society. In other words, the assumption is that if minority peoples are not present in future works within the genre, it is because prejudice has been eliminated, and not because race, class, and sex discrimination still exist in the world in which movie producers could not be bothered to represent minorities. If Storm is silent and seemingly less powerful in her movie representation than she is in the comic books, Berger's commentary tells us, it is because she chooses to fight for humanity and support her mutant counterparts, thus allowing commentators, critics, and academics to ignore the fact that this is a reconstructed image whose creators may not want to highlight that one of the most powerful mutants within the universe is an oppressed Black woman.

Examining these issues within the genre, the collaborative weblog *Racialicious*, which "discus[ses] media coverage of the multiracial community," published a now unavailable article, which suggested that the idea of Black identity within the genre is difficult to reconcile within a xenophobic society: "Black women cannot live vicariously through Storm. She is the Black Fantasy [white writers] spent more than two decades telling us we could never be. The fantasy is useless, for there is no comfort in engaging it. The character only serves to remind us of how short Black women fall from the racist norms society demands we aspire to" (Lynn). Although these images have not been widely examined, they highlight that the issue of the presence of Black women triggers a routine battle within the comic book genre.

The important question, of course, is if there is racism, why do Black woman superheroes exist at all? There are many answers to this question, but two of the most important ones touch on the impact of stereotypes themselves in relation to Black women: to both suggest we are free in society (despite contrary evidence) and also to show that Black women are strong and do not need protection. Like the happy, doting mammy and the "save my powers until white people need them" magical Negro stereotypes, the Black woman superhero is created to protect white society from atoning for their sins against Black bodies. Unlike Superman, having Black female heroes—a group who is arguably one of the most oppressed—defending whiteness suggests that Black women are mutually not a threat, need to be contained, and that they are submissive if "good."

This chapter looks at the history behind stereotypes and how they impact superheroes. The history that's needed to fully conceptualize this topic has been condensed, and I hope I've done my job in offering my former professor an admirable critique in the previous and forthcoming chapters. She is interested in the way that history and social change impacts Black women and peoples. If nothing else, this book similarly emphasizes that the images created about minorities, particularly Black women, are every bit as important as the physical harm inflicted on our bodies—and in many ways, these stereotypes imply to society that our physical harm is acceptable and even necessary.

4

Storm

• • • • • • • • • • • • • • • • • • • •

The Comics

In 2017, Fireside Magazine did a report on the absence of Black writers and creators within speculative fiction (science fiction, horror, fantasy, and so on), called the *Black Spec Report*, as they had done in previous years. The report showed that although Black representation had doubled (going from 2 percent to about 4 percent), Black writers were still greatly underrepresented considering Black people make up 13 percent of the U.S. population, leaving the report to conclude that "[s]uch dramatic underrepresentation can't be mathematically explained by random factors."

This means that there is a zero percent chance that the lack of representation is random.

Let that sink in for a moment. According to the stats in this study, the absence of Black voices and narratives within genre fiction is, for lack of a better word, intentional. In other words, white people love white people. They love to create stories about themselves. They love to read and imagine themselves the heroes in stories about themselves. They, no doubt, love themselves. The problem, though, is that it comes at the expense of other writers, and the stories that those writers are not given the opportunity to tell.

So, I sit here staring at the blank page, and my job is to convince those of you inclined to care that it's important to have a diverse field to have a healthy future. But how do I do that? I could write an anecdote beguiling you with a tale about how the bias in publishing affects me. But I'm Black. And you, as these numbers have shown us, do not care about Black voices or experiences. Whites, it seems, do not want to read about fascinating, dramatic, or just plain interesting and fun stories unless they center whiteness. Instead, I'm going to use an old trick I saw in a movie once. I'm going to have you imagine that you, as a creator or scholar, sit down at your keyboard, as I am doing now, to pen a tale or article. However, first you must be aware of what image you want to portray, and the way others will perceive your contribution. Is it too "other" or exotic? You want to create a character after this amazingly interesting person you know, but she too is different? Will the markers that denote her character be too stereotypical for publication? Is she too strong? Too feisty? Too motherly? Too sexy? You see, if she's too sexy, she may be a jezebel, while if she's too motherly, she may be a mammy. Too feisty? She's a Sapphire, you know that angry woman that we're always hearing about. The one that Black women work so hard in real life not to project so that others won't get the "wrong idea" about us. You want to write about a Black man? Make sure you stay away from the Buck, Mandingo, and magical Negro stereotypes, just to name a few. In fact, why do not you just dig out your copy of *Toms, Coons, Mulattoes, Mammies, and Bucks* and scan the whole 433-page volume to make sure you're not doing more harm than help to your community? After all, there were only thirty-one stories published by people that look like you in the 365 days that made up all of 2016. You cannot fuck this up.

Oh, but you thought you just wanted to spin a tale or write an article.

Now for the trick. As in that famous scene from a recent movie that shocked a courtroom in the film and the audience watching the screen, I want you to imagine that you have done all these things and you are *white*. That's right, as a white person, you need to be hyperaware of your race in every single circumstance imaginable, you must represent your race because there are shockingly few stories considered acceptable enough to appear before audiences that do not include your race, and you must, above all else, remember that you are *different*. You are not like those who will judge your work for acceptable "quality." And do not forget, it is our duty (above all else) to entertain the dominant race, and their sensibilities, whatever they may be.

But you remember that scene, do you not—the one from *A Time to Kill* (1996)? Where both jury members and moviegoers had to be tricked into thinking a Black body was worth defending? Fortunately, here—within this book—we do not have the trick of the camera to show a swollen, broken Black body or face. Even if we did the image might not shock you, since the advent of the Internet and camera phones have shown broken Black bodies on our computer screens and in our news cycles practically daily. And let's be honest, much of white America treats it as entertainment to pick over the wrongdoings of the dead Black person. It's like a game, similar to one your grandparents and great grandparents played, which included feasting under the poplar trees adorned with strange fruit.[1]

But I am a Black scholar, writer, and Afrofuturist, and this is often what we do—use history and our cultural understanding to examine the present and imagine a future. Our stories are different from yours and are unique in ways that are often difficult for you to engage. But no worries, you are a white creator and fan or scholar (or both), and evidence shows that white people love stories about white people. And true to my word, this is a story about white people. Or at least, it is about white writers, fans, and scholars. You see you did not have to imagine any of these things before you sat down to write. When the sage advises you to write what you know, you can do that and be relatively certain that you know whiteness, from the center— as a normal state of being. It is natural to you. It is acceptable. To you, it is even good. You know if your story is not chosen, that it is not because you are white. That may not stop you from getting upset, however. After all, thirty-one stories out of the 1089 published in 2016 were basically "affirmative action stories." Right? We've all heard it before: those Black people did not deserve to be published, and you, white writer/scholar, who may even have written a damn good piece, have been robbed of your rightful place in the publishing world by one of those thirty-one stories.

I jest only slightly; if you have been paying any attention to genre works for the last few years, you know this is no laughing matter. But this discussion does not compare you to your grand-persons who lynched my grand-persons in a tree. Admittedly, that is over the top.

No, contemporary white people who ignore injustice are more akin to the spectator who sat and watched without lifting a finger to help. While no one will die in the writing of this book nor, perhaps, due to the lack of Black people in genre publishing, the death of culture and voice and understanding of peoples different from you cannot be overstated. Do not underestimate the power that you have to simply engage (purchase, read, discuss) with publications that offer critical discourse on racially disenfranchised groups and topics.

The speculative fiction genre has a lot in common with comics and there is, in fact, a lot of overlap. Many writers who began as fiction writers are comic writers, and many are still working in both fields. Examples are Jim Starlin (*The Infinity Gauntlet*), Neil Gaiman (*Miracleman* and the iconic Sandman series published by Vertigo) and John Byrne ("Dark Phoenix Saga" and "Days of Future Past" storylines in the X-Men series). I could go on and on listing writers that work in both genre fiction and comics, but this is not the only connection between the two. Another natural overlap is the one between the supernatural and the superhero. Both rely heavily on the absurd, the fantastical, and suspension of disbelieve. Likewise, the mystical is present in both genres.

We have discussed how the creation of stereotypes around Black bodies is detrimental to real Black bodies within society, and the aforementioned Fireside 2017 report and subsequent anecdote also show that the ability to create fantastical stories of heroes and foes—good and evil—lies almost solely within the hands of white creators. Those hands mold the stories of the heroes of whiteness, at the expense of Black and other minority people.

While race is an important factor when studying Storm, as discussed in chapter 2, gender is just as paramount to her construction as a character that is both Black and a woman. In direct connection to the previous chapters, this chapter works to add to the existing analysis of the Negro spiritual woman while applying the analysis to Storm. The discussion shows that the character is given magical powers that were never meant to offer her freedom from the white social structure, but also that her powers are contained, and thus are not enough to change her status in the world, keeping her controlled so that her Black, female body does not upset the status quo.

History of Storm

Debuting around what was arguably the Black feminist revolution of the 1970s, Storm was a new breed of superhero. She is Black, a woman, and powerful enough to control the weather. As the longest running Black female superhero character, Storm has been reimagined many different times, including as a vampire. She has spawned her own series, as well as appeared in many other character series. Storm is one of the most recognized characters within the comic book world and is arguably one of the only recognizable Black female comic book characters in the mainstream.

Storm, whose birth name is Ororo Munroe, is descendant of a long line of African priestesses. She has stark white hair and dark skin, has the power to control the weather both on this planet and outside of it, and she is considered a mutant—an Omega level mutant—meaning the upper levels of her powers are unknown. This makes her one of the most powerful beings on the planet. Although Storm's mother is an African princess, she moved to the United States after marrying a photojournalist named David Monroe. Storm is born in New York, but her parents move to Cairo when she is just six months old. At five, Storm loses her parents when a plane crashes into their home; she becomes an orphan.

Soon, Storm is taken in by a group of street kids who train her to pick pockets and locks, and to steal. It is during this time that Storm first meets Charles Xavier, a mutant with telepathic powers, as she tries, and fails, to rob him. After being forced to kill a man who tries to rape her, Storm swears to herself that she will never take another human life.

Storm eventually travels to her homeland, Kenya, where a woman takes her in and teaches her to use her powers responsibility. Soon, local tribes begin to worship her as a goddess, and she protects them from outside forces and invaders with her powers.

Later, Xavier enlists her to join the X-Men, a group of mutants who fight to maintain peace between humans and mutants. It is then that he explains to her that she is not a "goddess" but a mutant and that she has a responsibility to protect the world, as much as her local community. After accepting his offer, Ororo is given the codename Storm, and forever becomes an X-Man. Eventually, Storm is appointed leader of the X-Men, and later has a short marriage to Black Panther, another Black character in the Marvel universe.

This chapter examines four separate comic series in which Storm is the main character and will briefly touch on the first issue in which she first appears, *Giant-Size X-Men* #1 from 1975. These particular issues feature Storm as a title character and follow her story, allowing us to examine the way the character is portrayed when given the opportunity to "star" in her own series. The discussion also looks at the degree to which Storm conforms to or subverts the controlling images of the magical Negro, the mammy, and others. The issues include *Uncanny X-Men* (1975) *Uncanny X-Men* #185, #186 (*Lifedeath*), and #198 (*Lifedeath II*), *Ororo Before the Storm* (#1–4), the Gene Nation series (*Storm* #1–4), *Make It Rain* (*Storm* vol. 1), and *Bring the Thunder* (*Storm* vol. 2).

To historically position the 1975 comic in which Ororo makes her first appearance, the *Combahee River Collective Statement*, which is written by Black women feminists, and denounces the "pejorative stereotypes attributed to Black women" that have caused us harm and seeks to focus on eliminating "our own oppression," comes out two years later (Combahee River Collective). Note that by this time in the mid-seventies and for some time before, Black women have named and begun to denounce the images that are harmful and negatively impact our lives.

True or not (it is debated), there is a well-known belief that Stan Lee modeled X-Men after the Civil Rights Movement of the 1960s, and particularly leaders such as Malcolm X and Martin Luther King. The story goes that Lee was so sympathetic to the racial oppression of Black people during the Civil Rights era that he used "mutantism" to symbolize the racism of Black and minority people around the world. In a video found on YouTube, he states that "the only things [Marvel doesn't] have room for [is] hatred, intolerance, and bigotry" (Marvel Entertainment, "A Message from Stan Lee"). This is commendable. To be clear, however, even if there is a semblance of truth to the stories and even if Lee's desire to be inclusive and represent oppressed groups may be notable, in execution it is flawed and even creates new problems for the groups depicted. We will not spend a lot of time defending or decrying Lee (or other creators within the Marvel Universe), as this is not about any one person but instead is about the ways in which stereotypes are created and recreated over time and how we each can recognize and reject them as they appear.

Uncanny X-Men (1975)

Written by comic writer Linda Fite, the plot of *Giant-Size X-Men* #1 is that the original X-Men have gone missing, and Charles Xavier (Professor X) and Cyclops seek out new mutants through Cerebro, a machine meant to detect humans and particularly mutants around the world, to help them find the lost crew. The new cast consist of eight new mutants, including an Asian man, Sunfire; a Native man, renamed (against his will) Thunderbird; and Ororo, renamed Storm. This is arguably the largest nonwhite cast readers have seen within the X-Men series to date.

The first clear image of Storm depicts her standing at an altar where the native people of Kenya are coming to pay her homage and beg her to help them with their crops. She is clearly darker skinned than the other white characters that have been shown, though in this panel she is in shadow and her skin has an orange tint. She is only wearing a loincloth over her mid-section and her long white hair is covering her breasts. There is energy flying around her and she is obviously powerful. Her subjects call her "Goddess" and worship her as a deity. She also respects them, calling them "my children." It has not rained in this area of Kenya; and the drought is ruining the crops and the people offer her cattle in return for making it rain. She refuses their gifts because they "need them more" than she does, but grants their wish, bringing winds and rains with the mere wave of her hands (Wein).

As she lifts her arms "her liquid eyes grow dark then—and the sky grows dark as well (emphasis from the comic)" (Wein). Storm's original eye color is "crystal blue" and every time she uses her power, they turn black. In this moment, Storm's "Blackness" is bubbling under the surface—uncontained—and her eyes are the windows through which the audience glimpse the dangerous power within this Black, female body. This is an example of the "bad is black effect" archetype. Coined by scholars Adam L. Alter, Chadly Stern, Yael Granot, and Emily Balcetis, the bad is black effect posits that Blackness is associated with perceptions of evil. Throughout history, white people have needed to justify enslaving and oppressing Black people, and to do this, Blackness was connected to wickedness, immorality, and evilness.

Much of Christianity's "mark of Cain" and the "curse of Ham" have been interpreted as God having given Black people the "curse" of dark skin so that others will know that they have been marked—and thus how to treat them. Throughout history this has been used to rationalize the oppression of Black people. Associating Blackness with a curse from God does not just suggest that Black-skinned people are evil, but it makes this bigotry ordained and substantiated by God Himself. Within this doctrine, the children of Cain and Ham (Black, cursed people) have to atone for their sins against God by being subordinate and in service to whites. Oppressing Black people, then, is not about white oppression of Black bodies, but about God—and who are you to disobey God?—instead justifying Black oppression as

Uncanny X-Men (1975).

Uncanny X-Men (1975).

natural and good. This is a construction that has lasted throughout different denominations of Christianity and was only denounced in some sects as recently as the 1980s.[2] However, the idea has persisted and does not only hold religious connotations, as the bad is black effect shows. Storm's Black skin and her eyes becoming dark when she uses her power play on the fears that there is inherently a darkness within Black people, particularly Black women—as women are also constructed as witches, evil, and wicked.

While whiteness is good and pure and Blackness is bad and evil, Charles Xavier wants to harness Storm's power for what he calls the "real" world, what he clearly sees as "goodness." Charles tells Ororo that the world she lives in, and the people she protects are a "beautiful . . . fantasy" while working to force her into serving him and white people at large. Without reviewing the magical Negro trope, it should be understood that this will be Storm's fate throughout the series. At this point, it is surprising when she is *not* constructed as the MN. What is more surprising is what Xavier says next. Charles tells Ororo that not only is she delusional and living in a "fantasy" but that she "is no Goddess" and instead "is a mutant [with] responsibilities" (Wein). In this moment, the reader must ask themselves: how is Storm not fulfilling her responsibilities to her people already? The only way that what Xavier says to her makes sense is if we accept that the Black people Storm have sworn to protect are not seen as people at all to Xavier.

Quite simply, Professor X is "negging" Ororo. For those not familiar, negging is when someone, usually a man, gives a backhanded compliment to someone else, usually a woman, to coax them into submission. As of 2022, there are whole men's empowerment manuals and websites devoted to helping men manipulate women through negging. Negging is based on the premise that any man can "knock any woman down a peg" to damage her self-esteem, so that she won't think so highly of herself, and the man can get whatever he wants from her. In real life, this usually happens in the context of a date or a more nefarious gender-based encounter, but in the world of the X-Men, Xavier uses it to interrupt Storm's confidence, causing her to question herself. Ororo, Charles suggests, is powerful (the compliment), but not quite as powerful as she thinks (the backhandedness: she is not a goddess), and as such, she should follow him so that he can train her to be a better person, teaching her "real responsibility." This is meant to give Charles full control over Ororo and puts him in a powerful position over her, allowing him to take ownership over her powers.

While negging was coined in 2004 or so, it is not new. It is no surprise that a white male character from the 1970s is using it against a Black woman, and that it is seen as inconsequential. What is surprising is that this is written by a white (or white presenting) woman. Instead of assuming this detail to be extraneous, however, we should see this emotionally manipulating behavior from a supposed "good guy" in the initial moments of meeting Storm as indictive of the way that Black women superhero characters must navigate spaces of white supremacy.

Pushing this a step further, Xavier is by all accounts a smart and educated man. He understands that words are simply representative of the people who use them. So, in this case, why would he even suggest that his word for describing the superpowers that they all possess ("mutants") is somehow more appropriate than the word that Storm and her people use ("Goddess")? The only reason for him to do this, yet again, is to insinuate that she is not as powerful and important as she thinks she is, so that she will be more likely to submit to him. While "Goddess" suggests a deity, a female god, within the world of X-Men, a mutant is just another reject that is oppressed. Ororo is not a reject, though, and she is not oppressed in this society and in this time. She is loved and adored and finds power in the people who have accepted her. Instead, Charles enters her world, shatters her self-esteem, and makes her just another oppressed mutant.

Moreover, we must question Charles's idea of responsibility. Is Ororo not fulfilling her responsibilities to her people by helping them to sustain their community, by bringing rain, by offering them hope? Again, this is completely illogical unless we accept that the Black people that Storm have sworn to protect are not constructed as people in the X-Men world. Patrick Brantlinger states that "Africa grew 'dark' as Victorian explorers, missionaries, and scientists flooded it with light, because the light was refracted through an imperialist ideology that urged the abolition of 'savage customs' in the name of civilization" (166). In the text, the Black Africans' bodies dance naked in the rain (*Giant-Size X-Men* #1), reminiscent of the way people from the constructed *dark continent* have been depicted within a white supremacist lens for centuries—as savages who are not capable of taking care of themselves, who are ignorant enough to believe in heathen Gods, and who, more importantly, do not deserve protection in the same ways that white people do.

It is not surprising that a white woman is upholding white supremacist ideologies in opposition to supposed feminist ideas of sisterhood. As a testament to the mindset of white authority within the series, Ororo is written so that she does not once question the mentally abusive man before her. Instead, she says: "You present a most peculiar argument. . . . I will come with you." In this moment, the Negro spiritual woman is strong, submissive, and silent. She does not speak out against the ideas that Xavier presents as she is constructed as the "good" Black woman who is wild, and needs to not only be tamed, but brought down from her own high ideas of herself. She is taken from the wild, "dark" continent of Africa to be placed within the absolute control of the white man who can contain her. As signified by her black eyes, an out-of-control Storm would threaten the whole world, but a tame one who can be used for the good of the white protagonists is the only acceptable role for a woman with the uncontrollable power that Ororo possesses.

The *Storm* Series (1996)

Written by British comic book writer Warren Ellis, this series focuses on the title character, who has been appointed leader of the X-Men. Questioning her leadership abilities and upset over having had to kill a member of Gene Nation, she performs a ceremony in the sewer system to remember the dead but is transported into another dimension where survival of the fittest and Darwinism[3] is the only way to exist. The Gene Nationals have evolved into a brutal group who battle and kill each other to make it up The Hill to their leader, Mikhail Rasputin.

At the beginning of this series, Storm is questioning her own ability to lead the X-Men. She has been forced to "cut out a little girl's heart" because the child was a Morlock who had a "bomb attached to [her heart]" (Ellis, *Storm* #1). Storm speaks to several of the male protagonist mutants, who tell her that she has done what she had to do to survive and protect the world and that she should not question herself. While admitting that she is a competent leader ("I'm not a bad leader. I know it"), she still feels compelled to go into the sewers to perform a ceremony honoring the dead mutants, the Gene Nationals, that have died there under her leadership (Ellis, *Storm* #1). Of course, the other, male mutants within this series do not struggle over the choices that they have made, including Storm's co-leader, Cyclops, who has also killed other mutants, but is not fraught over having been forced to do so. Instead, Storm herself seems to struggle with what is often considered part of the job, perhaps because she is a woman. However, this need not be understood as completely negative. Connecting to her ancestral religion that does not represent Christianity (which, as previously mentioned, has historically been harmful for Black people) offers Storm a moment of subversion of the status quo of Westernized religion. Likewise, very often Black characters struggle to prove their "humanity within a world that vilifies them," so to see Storm struggling with obvious human traits of regret and sympathy could very well be another point of subversion for the character (Brooks, "Finding the Humanity in Horror" 14).

Similarly, when Storm is transported to The Hill, she learns that Mikhail Rasputin wants her to "mother" the demented mutants, the Gene Nationals, so that they can learn what a true fighter should be. When conceptualizing what "the mammy" looks like for Storm in this book, it's clear that the artists did not construct Storm as a mammy figure at the beginning of this series. In fact, she is expected to be ruthless and brutal to her new "children" so that they in turn can become such. This is the opposite of the archetypal mammy, who is expected to mother and protect white children over her own.

However, by the end of the series, the mammy imagery is apparent. Once Storm and the X-Men have beaten Rasputin and many of his evil mutants, several of the Gene Nationals remain. Unsure of what to do with them, Storm quickly decides to send them to Africa. "I have a harsh environment for you," she tells them, "A village in Africa, gone to ruin through short-termism" (Ellis, *Storm* #4). While Storm's concern is the people within the United States, and the fear that letting these dangerous mutants loose on the populace is real, she decides to place them with African peoples who are even less likely to be able to protect themselves from the mutants. Although Storm warns them that she "will be watching," this is no solution for the very real threat that these beings could create for the weakened people within this region (Ellis, *Storm* #4).

Keeping Toni Morrison's "white creator" ideology in mind, the author expects the reader to believe that Storm is protecting the people of Africa by sending the Gene Nationals to farm the land and help the people, despite their propensity toward violence. It is also important to note that the Gene Nationals are being sent to a ravaged region whose people cannot protect themselves against these vicious beings if they decide to wreak havoc. Clearly, here, Storm is behaving as a mammy, protecting her white "children" of the United States, while neglecting the danger posed to her own "children" of Africa.

Furthermore, Storm's sexuality is so powerful within the series, it's overwhelming for men: "Abruptly Cable becomes aware of Storm's scent. It's not like a perfume, but a natural sandalwood, musky and uncomplicated" (Ellis, *Storm* #1). Storm's "earthly" scent is often commented on in this series by Cable. Her natural musky scent implies that she is not only "uncomplicated" but also closer to nature and thus more carnal, more animalistic. In this way, Storm is portrayed as sensual and venereal, through the white male's lust for her. Similarly, Storm's scent is an embodiment of her own sexuality that is not only projected in the image of her (arm raised, caressing her hair; large erect breasts), but also through her sexuality that tempts the white male character, Cable.

Storm (1996). Storm becoming sexy for the male gaze.

This objectification is complete at the end of the series when Cable catches another whiff of Storm's scent as she enters the room, having undergone a makeover. The new Storm has cut her hair and adorns herself with more revealing clothes, including an exposed midriff. All of the men are in awe, their mouths hanging open, while she poses for them, hands on hips, saying, "Well, my old uniform was ruined, and I felt like a change. Something that commands the attention a little more" (Ellis, *Storm* #4). Despite everything that Storm has accomplished within this series, the ending relies so heavily on her appearance that all her other accomplishments are thrown aside in favor of the white male gaze. Despite her abilities, her powers, and her intellect, the message readers are left with, and the one that she herself exhibits, is that she values her sex appeal, her ability to attract (white) men, over everything else. The stereotype of the Negro spiritual woman is irrefutable; she is at once submissive, mysterious, and hypersexualized.

It can be argued that within this final scene Storm is in control of her own sexuality, and that this is simply a light-hearted way to end the series. However, her desire to attract white men's attention hearkens back to the jezebel, who is defined as sexually "insatiable" and promiscuous. Adding all these things together and taking into account our discussion in chapter 2, Storm seems to embody most of the real-life stereotypes of Black women in this series, coming full circle to the Negro spiritual woman.

As previous scholars have noted, it is impossible to divorce Black women's gender from their race. As such, when Storm decides to send the Gene Nationals to Africa, she is not only behaving as a mammy, but using her powers for the benefit of white society as a magical Negro would. The magical Negro's power is only used to empower and protect whiteness and the needs of the white character. In this instance, the United States is a proxy for whiteness, and Storm is protecting it despite the threat to her homeland, Africa. This works wholly to disrupt Blackness to benefit the status quo, thus earning her a place of recognition and acceptance into whiteness.

Scholars state that the magical Negro is the "noble, good-hearted black man or woman" who is "saintly" but is "morally equal to their White counterparts" (Glenn and Cunningham 138). This is no less true for Storm within this series. While she appears to be noble for protecting the United States and simultaneously helping Africa ("You will work the land, plant foods in dry soil and make the place live again," one of the X-Men tells the surviving Gene Nationals; Ellis, *Storm* #4), she is protecting America, which is majority white, while putting majority Black Africa in danger.

In the end, this allows the United States to uphold the American exceptionalism that is often present in comic books, implying that Africans have ruined their lands because of "short-termism" and need someone to fix it for them (Petty 3). The Gene Nationals are expected to work the land, plant food in dry soil, and make the place livable again (Ellis, *Storm* #4). But the important questions are not explored: Where will the food come from? If there is food to plant, why has it not been given to the people so that they can begin to rebuild? If the soil is dry, why has Storm not used her powers and connections to bring rain and other prosperity to the land?

With these questions, it is not difficult to see where Storm's allegiance lies and how the "Negro" within her is possibly only magical when it protects whiteness.

Ororo: Before the Storm Series (2005)

The author of this series, Marc Sumerak, has also written for Thor, Avengers, and Black Panther. As the title suggest, this series also follows the main character, Storm, as a little girl. After her parents die, Ororo is taken in by a group of homeless children who are led by Teacher, Achmed El-Gibar. Having been trained to steal and pick locks to survive, Ororo and two friends are chosen by Teacher to break into an ancient African tomb to steal an amulet that is supposed to give the bearer immortality. While in the tomb, the children awaken a guardian who recognizes Ororo as an important figure and who shows carvings of her "destiny."

Ororo: Before the Storm is unique in that it follows Storm (Ororo) as a young child growing up as an orphan in the streets of Cairo. Because of this, the character is thankfully not sexualized and is rarely "mammied." However, because the character is homeless and has no family, she has essentially taken on fellow homeless children as siblings and Achmed El-Gibar, a local thief, as a father-like figure. Within this group, Storm has become his "prized pupil in the arts of thievery" (Sumerak, *Ororo* #3). As such, Ororo's job is to steal food for the other children, her self-adopted siblings, at one point stating that she "would suffer far more if [she] knew [she] had left a friend behind" (Sumerak, *Ororo* #1). While this is noble and very well may simply

Ororo: Before the Storm (1995). X-Men on the walls of an ancient tomb (Sumerak).

be the act of a young girl who wants to hold on to any piece of familial connection that she can since her parents died, it also places an undue burden on the young Black girl. Since Ororo is a tough character, having taken care of herself since her parents died, she now is expected to care for an untold number of children as if their mother. Because Ororo is strong on her own, readers are content in the knowledge that she is capable of mothering an entire community of children. This behavior is often expected of mammy characters. However, this alone is not enough to claim she's constructed as such, and the series goes a long way to show her humanity—a characterization that Black women characters often do not get.

What is interesting for this series, remarkably, is that Ororo uses her powers for both her own and her adopted family's benefit, a subversive act that

Ororo: Before the Storm (1995). The guardian forecasting Storm's future oppression (Sumerak).

has not been present within the comic books we have examined thus far. However, after Ororo breaks into the tomb the Guardian shows her pictures of her future-self on the ancient wall and explains that she will "soar on the winds as a savior of [her] people" (Sumerak, *Ororo* #3). When Ororo explains that she is an orphan and that she does not have people, the Guardian explains "Not yet, perhaps. But you will find them someday and you will lead them to a brighter tomorrow" (Sumerak, *Ororo* #3). Then he reveals another wall on which Xavier, the leader of X-Men, and Cyclops, another X-Men member, are sketched.

One wonders why two white men from the United States are sketched upon the walls of an ancient African tomb. While Ororo is of African descent, raised in Africa, and will presumably fight for the lives of African people,[4] the two white male X-Men leaders are equally billed on these walls. Not only does this imagery work to contain Ororo, suggesting that she is no more important to Africa than the white men from the United States, but it also implies that she is destined to follow these men instead of seeking a destiny outside of the white structured space that they create for her. In essence, the writing is on the wall: Storm is meant to work with the X-Men, leaving behind her homeland of Africa. She is the quintessential Negro spiritual woman.

As a child, the comic book contains Ororo by showing her that her destiny, although important, lies in helping whites. Her future importance must be in a land other than Africa because she must be greater than that, as Africa is, as previously mentioned, historically conceptualized as the "dark" continent. While Storm's eyes grow dark with her powers always threatening to overtake her, whiteness offers her a "brighter" future, away from the darkness. Throughout the series, Ororo longs for "the nothingness to finally give way to something more" (Sumerak, *Ororo #1*). It is finally revealed within the pages of this series that "something more" for Ororo does not mean exploring her powers and fighting for the well-being of the colonized and stripped continent of Africa. Instead, it means that her powers are best used elsewhere, and not on those who need her most—as in the previous series when she is silent when she is taken from her home—and who have become her family, but for whites who would wield her power to support rather than subvert the status quo.

When it comes to the magical Negro for the young Ororo, the stereotype is absolute. The future Storm will not only "assist the white characters on their journeys," but she will put aside any journey of her own and make theirs her personal mission (Entman and Rojecki 111). While other X-Men characters also support the team in this way, as discussed in chapter 3, Storm's African and African American ancestry is in opposition to the X-Men's mission in a way that white characters' ancestry is not. Because Storm is Black, working with the X-Men is exploitive since she is supporting the very status quo that is oppressive to her as a Black woman.

Storm Series (2006)

Penned by crime writer Eric Jerome Dickey, this series follows Ororo before she has become a member of the X-Men. She is older than the child in the previous series, but not quite a woman at its start. Ororo is still a thief who has only now come on her period and meets T'Challa (Black Panther), and the two fall in love. However, poachers are after the pair, hoping not only to cash in on Storm's ability to control the weather, but on Wakanda's (Black Panther's nation) wealth.

Storm (Dickey; 2006) is perhaps the most complicated series that has been examined within this book so far. As discussed in much of the previously cited literature, within this series it becomes very difficult to separate the way that different stereotypes and images functions within Black women's and character's lives. The magical Negro becomes difficult to distinguish from the jezebel and the mammy, and each of them seems to bleed into the other, while they all encompass the Negro spiritual woman. For example, at one point in the series, Storm is discussing why and how to become a woman with other Black women of the region. She is told by another Black woman that she must have sex before she is a fully a woman and that she cannot understand true womanhood until she has been taken by a man. This sexist idea of womanhood allows men to be in control of women's sexuality and their bodies, while suggesting that any woman who does not submit to a man, such as gay women, cannot ever fully be women. Likewise, the other women within the image have submitted to men (one being pregnant, her large belly exposed), without having been married. In a previous scene this pregnant woman stands watching as her baby's father tries to sleep with Ororo. The Black women within the series that are conceptualized as seeking nothing but the loins of a man are shunned, while not doing so makes them less than women. Simultaneously, Ororo's Blackness cannot be removed from the scene as this ideology is presented as African wisdom that "true" African women must follow. As such, the mammy, jezebel, and magical Negro are all working within this scene.

Researchers state that "despite Black people's talents and abilities, they [are not thought to] know how to use [supernatural abilities] appropriately without someone to instruct them how to do so" (Glenn and Cunningham 150). This works in a very particular way for Storm as this series is written by Eric Jerome Dickey, the only Black writer examined within this book. At one point, she is shown how to use her powers by Black Panther after and specifically because the two have had sex. Ororo does not need to be taught how to use her powers because she is Black (after all, this series is written by a Black man), but because she is a woman and cannot control her powers properly until she has submitted to a man and thus her womanhood must be completely contained before she can fully recognize her ability.

Examining the magical Negro image offers a possible moment of subversion within this series. At the end of the series, after Storm and Black Panther have defeated the antagonist, and she has learned to control her powers, Ororo's powers are revealed to an African village. A young girl comes up to Storm and asks: "Are you a god?" (Dickey, *Storm* #6). Ororo does not answer. By not answering the girl, Ororo seems to accept the responsibility of being a god to her people, thus taking on the role of protecting them, but also accepting her powers fully. Likewise, it is arguable that within this scene she accepts that she is more than human, but also that she is more than simply a mutant, only meant to serve whites, supporting the white power structure. Instead, she seems to own being a god and everything that comes along with it: the power and the responsibility. This is an empowering, subversive moment for Storm.

Storm's sexuality is complicated within this series. In moments that Ororo is seemingly subversive, she is simultaneously subjugated either for herself or other Black women within the series. For example, at one point Ororo takes full ownership of her own sexuality and refuses to have sex with Black Panther simply because he is king. However, all the other women want him and practically throw themselves at his feet. Later, another woman is so jealous of Ororo's beauty that she tries to kill her. Because Ororo is depicted with white phenotypical features, the implication is that Black women without traditionally white features are jealous of women who possess them. This plays on the idea, of course, that whiteness is not only more beautiful, but that Black people are, first, so violent that they harm with impunity; and second, that even Black people recognize the superiority of the white aesthetic.

In these interactions, Ororo is often empowered and subversive, but the controlling images around other Black women—who do not have blue eyes and white, non-4C hair[5]—are simultaneously oppressed. So, while Storm is sometimes subversive, Black women who (more often than not) do not look like Storm are not.

Ororo's body is a place of disruption within the series. She has come on her "cycle" and one of the women explains to her that a girl's rite of passage "can only be reached through the loins of a man" (Dickey, *Storm* #3). Once she finally has sex with Black Panther she exclaims: "I have so much energy" (Dickey, *Storm* #4).

After that, Storm learns how to use and control her powers in a way that she never has, but it is specifically because her sexuality is controlled by Black Panther. He can wield her and mold her and yet her own control of that sexuality is not complete without him. This also plays into the idea that Black women's sexuality is so powerful that it must be contained, lest it become corrupted. It is true that before Storm has sex her powers were uncontrolled and appeared only when she was angry, but after discovering the power that lies between her legs her superpowers explode beyond measure. When Black Panther, a Black man, shows her how to use her own power (after sex she can control her powers to make it rain only on Black Panther), how to breathe and calm herself so that she is in control, the reader is assured that she is fully able to be the superhero that they expect from her—in that she is fully contained by Black masculinity, if not whiteness. Like Wonder Woman before her, Storm has proven in these moments that she is worthy to fight to support male supremacy. Although this is not specifically a jezebel or a magical Negro stereotype, it is clearly the Negro spiritual woman, as Storm is being constrained through her superpowers, race, and sexuality.

It quickly becomes clear that "race" and "gender," which often did not fit within the controlling images chosen for this book, were very important within this series. Some of the most subversive images are likewise often quite oppressive. For all of Storm's progress and power, her gender and race are repressive for her and when she manages to subvert oppression, it is often transferred to the other Black women characters.

An example of this is that Storm's appearance is often compared to whiteness as the standard of beauty and good. At one point Storm asks Black Panther what he sees in her and he says a "Beautiful white lioness" (Dickey, *Storm* #4). Throughout the series Storm is depicted as dark skinned. She is not white, only her hair is white. Yet somehow the Black male character connects her beauty to whiteness, ignoring her entire Black body as also beautiful. Although it can be argued that Black Panther is simply referring to Storm's mane as white, just as a lioness's mane can be white, it is worth noting that most lions are also not white, and thus this connection is not natural or even obvious. Instead, it is just as forced and unnatural as ignoring all of her Black skin when referring to her beauty.

Throughout each of the series, men are often Storm's teachers and the other Black women within this series are often jealous of her, one becoming so jealous she willingly works for white men against the Black group. Storm has Black male friends who support her, but the women seemingly accept that Storm is somehow "better" or more beautiful than they are, and it makes them violent and envious.

Considering that many images of Black women other than Storm in this series are negative, it is unsurprising that by the end of the 2006 *Storm* series, the true antagonist has become a Black female character. She is angry at Storm because her own father preferred the superhero over her and Black Panther chose her as his partner, and so she seeks to kill Storm. As we have discussed, Black women are subjugated through both their race and their gender, even in Africa. Thus, having a series in which a jealous Black woman

Storm (2006). Depiction of another Black female character (Dickey).

appears to be an antagonist for Storm ignores the power dynamics at play within Black women's lives.

The images of Black women, however, are not the only negative stereotypes within these series. Throughout, but specifically within *Storm* (Dickey; 2006), Africa and Africans in general are equated with thievery. In the first issue the following dialogue takes place while several African orphans try to convince Storm to steal a camera from a white man:

BLACK WOMAN You're so American.

STORM I'm African.

WOMAN But you're becoming lazy as the Americans. She's afraid.

STORM Am not!

WOMAN Ororo is not one of us. . . . Chicken. You're not of Mother Africa.

   (Dickey, *Storm* #1)

Within this dialogue, Africa is being compared to thievery. Ororo is lazy and a "chicken" like an American, because she does not take joy in stealing as the others arguably do. Ororo "earns [her] keep" by picking locks, but this is not enough for the group of Africans, who seem to take delight in thievery. Many Black people are depicted as evil, deviant, and simply out for money, and are willing to steal and even kill to get it. They are thieves and seek—within both series set in Africa—to corrupt Storm, who is more upstanding and honorable, arguably due to her proximity to whiteness. Storm seems to only steal and pick locks because she must help feed the children within her community, but other Black people are less honorable, wanting to steal from whites simply because it is depicted as being in their nature.

In these images, Ororo wonders if she can reach heaven by stealing, and knows that even the African gods are angered by her thievery. If Storm is not truly African because she is unwilling to steal, how also is she angering the gods—presumably African gods—by being a thief? Why have these Africans not grown up with the same understanding of "the gods" as she has? Why is Storm the only seemingly moral and upstanding person on this continent? It appears that Storm has adopted a code of ethics that the Africans around her do not possess. Storm is "good" because she regrets what she does, while the others arguably are not because they accept stealing as a way of life. Africa and Africans are corrupt and amoral, while Storm's whiteness has her constructed as upstanding and good.

Within this scene, Blackness is depicted negatively or in oppositions to whiteness. Here, as Storm is a thief and presumably tainted, she wears a Black "nappy" wig to cover her own white hair. She has stolen the wig right off a woman's head for no apparent reason at all, other than to feel more African, to connect to Africa or other Africans in some way. Perhaps, though, she is seeking to hide her identity, or to hide the shame that she feels behind a curtain of Blackness. In the wig, Blackness is literally covering whiteness, and only when it's removed does Storm begin to become "good" and discover her true self and explore her womanhood.

In the end, whiteness is a stand-in for good and Blackness is the evil force that must be thrown away, discarded like the cheap wig that is eventually torn away to reveal Storm's beautiful whiteness.

Storm: Make It Rain/Bring the Thunder (2015)

This series is written by comic book writer and film director Greg Pak. Rather than spend an exorbitant amount of time describing this series, we can let the back cover copy speak for itself:

> Thief. Goddess. Headmistress. Queen. The X-Man called Storm has always defied a single title. And her desire to better the world has never been limited to only her own kind. On an ongoing mission to foster goodwill, and safeguard both mankind and mutants, Ororo Munroe will travel the globe—confronting villains, gods, monsters and everything in between. She will overthrow tyrants, quell tsunamis and strive to see her dream for the world realized. She is Storm, a hero like no other—and the skies will tremble at the sight of their namesake. But now, Storm must handle the fallout caused by familiar faces from her past. Why is Callisto kidnapping wayward youths from the streets of New York? Will Storm's romance with Forge be reignited? And can Yukio help Storm deal with the death of Wolverine? (Pak, *Make It Rain*)

In this series, Storm is the leader of the X-Men and for the Jean Grey School for Higher Learning, which teaches young mutants how to use their powers responsibility and safely. She spends the first part of the series quelling a tsunami outside the United States in the fake city of Santo Marco, much to the adoration of the inhabitants, particularly a young Black girl who runs into her arms and holds her tightly. The rest of the series follows her as she seeks to save and protect people (generally children or young people, but also fellow mutants) from other groups that are growing ever more violent. Storm struggles, not with the responsibility of running the X-Men, but with when and where her loyalties should lie—at one point struggling with the choices of her dead lover Wolverine's decisions to ally himself "with monsters and murders."

While Storm wrestles with her choices in the series, you will notice that the cover copy of the comic whittles it down to one line: "her desire to better the world has never been limited to only her own kind." By only "her kind," the text means "Black people." In other words, Storm's heroism is established because she fights for white people, and "not just" Black people. It is important for the creators of the comic to make this clear even before a single page has been opened. The problem, of course, is as Toni Morrison addresses in an interview with Charlie Rose in 1989: the implication that Storm must focus on someone other than Black people suggests that Black "lives [have] no meaning or depth without the white gaze" (Rose). The case has often been made that white people not only understand the bigger picture, but they, by definition, are the bigger picture. Thus, centering whiteness becomes necessary for Black and other marginalized groups, and the fight against injustice rarely includes race. If Black heroism centered the fight for racial justice in a transformative way, then that fight would be against the very white people who are reading, writing, and publishing these works. This could never happen in our current political climate. Instead, race—or rather, racism—is presented as a hinderance for Storm, and her people become a burden in a way that whites and whiteness never are for white superheroes.

The series' depiction of race and power dynamics is compelling. Storm is clearly in charge, but she also negotiates her authority with an unknown "they" and even uses her power against minority people when threatened. At one point a young student at the school named Marisol Guerra (code-name Flourish), a brown-skinned Mexican girl, is upset that she has been taken from her family and "community" (Pak, *Make It Rain*). She is bullied by the other students and called "Creep" because of her powers of chlorokinesis, the ability to make plants or vegetation grow. Arriving home after stopping the tsunami, Storm tells Marisol that the school is a place where mutants "can be accepted" (Pak, *Make It Rain*). But Marisol is not

Make It Rain / Bring the Thunder (2015) (Pak).

having it, telling Storm that she has no right to pull kids out of their homes, "indoctrinating them in mutant ideology" (Pak, *Make It Rain*). The story does not explain what "mutant ideology" is, but I do not think it is a stretch to say that it not far from some of this book's arguments, particular in relation to forcing mutants into a submissive role that supports the white power structure. Marisol goes on to accuse Storm of being led by what "Xavier told" her instead of her own ideas. The younger girl argues that Storm and the entire school are "framed as people of tremendous privilege gifting things to the poor," and ends by calling Storm a "sellout." Storm does not respond to this in words and instead she causes a weather front to come into the room, knocking the girl on her butt and drenching her in water.

Let's be clear here, when confronted with very real concerns, Storm uses her powers against not only another mutant, but against another nonwhite person. Storm's anger is likely because the girl is right: the older woman has adopted a colonialist mindset in which minority people's cultures, lack of wealth, and race are weaponized against them. The white savior complex is an identity that white people often adopt, falsely claiming to help nonwhite people for personal gain—even when the gain is simply for their own ethical or political dogma. While Storm is not white, her ideologies, as Marisol suggests, are harmful and mirror whiteness.

In her article in the *New Criminal Law Review*, Jessica Swanson states that:

> By Western standards, otherness or holding a different set of values and beliefs is considered to be a savage construct, and any place in the world that is inherently different—whether in culture, politics, religion, or the color of individual's skin—falls into this category. Desperation in these "other" places often is the result of tenuous survival. [...] The concept of the white savior reaching out to save these victims is invalidated when these saved victims are returned. (600)

While Swanson is referring to human trafficking, the general message is the same, and a broader argument can be made that Xavier and the school are trafficking in mutant bodies. Storm is angry because Marisol would rather be home with her family in possible poverty than to be in the place that Storm and those like her think is a safer space for the child. In his article "Childhood Indoctrination for Minority-Group Membership," Joshua A. Fishman states that the minority-group child is expected to be "attracted to [the American core culture], surrender willingly to it, [and] desire to participate fully in it" (330). Marisol does not want these things; thus, she is constructed in this moment as "bad" and Storm's Black body is charged with getting her back in line—like a mammy. Storm's faux desire to protect the girl is borne out of her own support of white supremacy's tendency to "other" minority groups, rather than any genuine need to help and protect her. Whereas this is also a white American mindset that positions the United States of America as the "best country on earth," the ideology can also be framed through a more modern incarnation of the (more often than not) white American woman: The Karen.

Many of us will have seen this white women's relentless desire to control Black and minority bodies (while claiming to be protecting) in viral videos recently within our culture. This construction is identified as the "Karen" and/or "momma bear" images that white women often engage order to defend their aggressive actions. For the last few years, the Karen has entered U.S. popular culture as a term for a (usually) white, entitled women who is demanding beyond the point of reason and who works to force marginalized groups, often Black women, back into a place that makes the Karen more comfortable. Videos of white women screaming at and calling the police on Black and other marginalized people for no reason, other than that they want to be able to control Black and minority bodies, permeate social media.

The Karen archetype is directly connected to the self-created image that many white women have conceptualized around themselves as the "momma bear." This image seems to allow adult women to believe that their angry, aggressive behavior is strength; that it is power. Coupled with the numerous films about white women who fight against massive odds to beat anyone and anything to supposedly protect their young (*The Blind Side* [2009], for example) momma bears are constructed as heroes, or at least powerful enough to make change, if only for themselves and their loved ones. The persona of the "Mama grizzly bear" entered the U.S. canon with Sarah Palin in 2010. Scholars have said it was a way for her to "blend [her] feminine and masculine qualities and capabilities," and this is true (Burns 688). But it also allowed Palin to create an image of herself as a strong (and even violent, if needed), formidable opponent. Momma bears are Karens who scream at strangers in the street, attack others, and play victim, knowing they will not get harmed—not because they're dangerous like bears, but because white femininity is protected in society and they know they will not be harmed. Now by all accounts, Storm is not a Karen—she has an unparalleled amount of power that she is, in at least some cases, able to control and use for marginalized groups—but in aggressively attacking Marisol with her powers, she is acting and behaving in a way that mirrors the white womanhood exhibited by most Karens. The problem for Storm, of course, is that she is not a white woman, and as we have seen throughout this book, she too often does not have the privilege of white womanhood. The only reason this works for her in this moment is because she is conforming to whiteness and invoking white supremacist ideas. Storm, as a Black woman "from the streets," like Marisol, should understand the truth that the girl speaks. She has every opportunity to listen to the child's concerns and address them, if only to console her in a mostly white space that does not accept her. Storm understands what this feels like, being a dark-skinned woman with white hair.

In this way, it is apparent that Storm's "mutant-ness" and Blackness are always at odds, and her previous socioeconomic class should put her in a unique position to understand Marisol like no other person in that school. Instead, although Storm eventually apologizes to the girl at the end of the series, it is Henry, Storm's second in command, who contacts Marisol, apologies to her, and extends another invitation to come back and be a part of the X-Men, only after Storm has physically attacked this brown-skinned child.

One of the most inspiring things about the series is that it is possible to see that growth of progressive social norms around Blackness has evolved to at least some degree. One example is the way Marisol calls Storm out on her indoctrination of whiteness, as mentioned above. This did not happen in previous series critiqued here. But throughout the 2015 series, there are moments of disruption to the narrative of whiteness that is both notable and refreshing. Logan (Wolverine) dies at the beginning of the series, and although Storm is tasked with filling his shoes, she rejects what (she believes) he did to end the conflict, searching out a better way that is more suitable for her, as a Black woman. More importantly, Logan's love for Storm is apparent, and though she is sexually desired by many of the men in the series, she is not necessarily sexualized as the jezebel in the 2015 series. No one "smells her scent," for example. As for the mammy, Storm spends a lot of time helping children in the series, at one point searching for a little white girl who is missing, but she is not constructed as the doting Black domestic to white children, content in servitude. She, for all intents and purposes, is not the mammy here. There are several positive aspects of the character here that we have not seen in the Storm stories before this.

Small steps, however, are not enough to escape from the oppressive spaces in which Storm finds herself within the series. Many will argue that at least some progress has been made and still others will suggest that we scholars who do this kind of work should be happy with the little amount of progress that has been made. But, first, expecting someone to endure a particular kind of oppression that you, personally, would never experience, is problematic to the degree that this book is likely not for you anyway; and second, I refer you to Rev. Dr. Martin Luther King Jr.'s "Letter from a Birmingham Jail."

Martin Luther King Jr.'s "I Have a Dream" speech is often used by white people seeking to shut down Black voices. I know this from personal experience. At a conference in September 2019, I got onto a "debate" with a random white guy over the idea that nonviolence is always the correct answer. He tried to trot out Martin Luther King (MLK), of course. So, I hit him with "Letter from a Birmingham Jail," in which MLK posits that he has:

almost reached the regrettable conclusion that the Negro's great stumbling block in the stride toward freedom is not the White Citizens Councillor or the Ku Klux Klanner but the white moderate who is more devoted to order than to justice; who prefers a negative peace which is the absence of tension to a positive peace which is the presence of justice; who constantly says, "I agree with you in the goal you seek, but I can't agree with your methods of direct action"; who paternalistically feels that he can set the timetable for another man's freedom; who lives by the myth of time; and who constantly advises the Negro to wait until a "more convenient season." Shallow understanding from people of good will is more frustrating than absolute misunderstanding from people of ill will. Lukewarm acceptance is much more bewildering than outright rejection. (3)

The quote is an obvious condemnation of this man and his ideologies toward forced pacifism of Black people. He did not like me quoting King in a way that does not fit his limited, controlled image of the man. Like many white people who use MLK to deflect Black people, he had not read "Letter," as it does not support his ideas of a passive Black leader that he can use to silence unruly Blackness.

But there I was, a smart Black woman who was a guest, a scholar, and knew her shit, so instead of acknowledging that he might not completely understand the ideologies of a man who he likely only encountered in third grade history class, he said, "I'm using an academic argument here." Not an academic himself, he wasted no time insinuating that he is more academically sound solely due to his whiteness and propensity to argue with Black women over our rejection of a white-constructed "nonviolence" doctrine— perhaps more appropriately, our failure to play the "good" mammy to make him comfortable. But to him I am an angry Black woman, and it was his social responsibility to make sure I was contained. I had been reasoned and even toned while he constantly interrupted me and leaned in uncomfortably close, invading my space. But he had a penis and a giant handlebar mustache, so society tells him that he is "logical," and that same society tells him that I, a Black woman, am emotional and uneducated.

I can play this game, I thought. I looked at him, used my academic voice and said clearly: "I am using critical race theory, feminist theory, and Marxist theory to support my assertions. Exactly what academic scholarship are you using to support yours?" Said gentleman, of course, did not have a response because he was not actually using any such framework—not because there is no academic framework in which to place a post–MLK white, constructed passive image, but because it was painfully clear that this man was simply seeking to shut down my voice and extensive research on the topic. His discomfort and response are meant to disrupt my understanding of my own Blackness, so that he can control his own understanding of his whiteness.

There are many people who argue that if Black people would just "play nice" that somehow, magically, whites will become amendable to Black suffering and end racism. White people love MLK now that he's dead because they want to believe he was passive. Yet, in his time he was not popular (never receiving more than about a 45 percent popularity rating; by comparison, he has over 90 percent now), and then he was murdered—by a white man.

If nothing else, this anecdote suggests that many white people will do anything to keep from dealing with racial injustice, including rewriting an entire Black man's image to make him just passive enough for them to stomach. If this can happen to *the* Martin Luther King Jr.—a real man whose words were some of the most disseminated from his time and who is one of the most quoted men of his era—what exactly does this look like for a Black woman character who is written, created, and imagined from a mind of mostly white men?

Conclusion

While I love scholarship, research, and writing, my heart in many ways is in the classroom. I adore teaching and I love having the opportunity to offer students the critical thinking skills they need to navigate the world. My teaching and scholarship philosophy are derived largely from my understanding of the ways in which people learn and exist within society. While my minor in education has afforded me the opportunity to read a myriad of texts that have been fundamental in shaping my understanding of the educational system, such as *Pedagogy of the Oppressed* (1968), *Miseducation of the Negro* (1933) and *The Shame of the Nation* by Jonathan Kozol (2005), it was shadowing a professor in grad school that helped form my pedagogical identity. Teaching an Intro to African American Studies class, the professor asked the students: "If given the opportunity to learn unquestionable knowledge about God, would you take it?" I was shocked to learn that only a handful of students out of nearly a hundred would willingly accept that knowledge. This suggests three things to me:

1 That people know their ideologies are flawed and possibly constructed.
2 If given the choice, they'd maintain their false ideologies rather than change, out of fear.
3 People directly relate their ideologies with their own existence. In other words, people are their ideologies and vice versa.

Armed with this knowledge, I realized that dictating my views would never be an effective strategy for me. I gathered that some people "learn" to play the game by memorizing information but garner little understanding of the subject matter. As such, standardized testing, especially within humanities, is not an indicator of actual knowledge learned or of analytical accruement. Instead, I believe that we each construct our own reality from our beliefs (often learned in childhood), and any information that we come in contact with along the way we add to an already existing ideological structure to make sense in our own lives. In other words, we learn by building on top of the knowledge we already have and often resist throwing aside false information that is part of that knowledge.

Questions help us construct knowledge. Consequently, the more questions we ask, the more ways we can index thoughts in our memories. I have found that students tend to lose some or all intrinsic fascination once extrinsic motivators, like grades, are gone. Therefore, I work very hard to take the motivation of grades away and make it about student's own existence within society. This is what I have likewise worked to do within this book. Offering pop culture references (negging) and current social examples (the Karen) makes even historical literature and other topics relevant in most people's lives. In this way, we are all responsible for our own education, and some of the most valuable lessons in life are the ability to form an analysis and make sense of the society around us.

This, in essence, is what *Hero Me Not* seeks to do. Examining both the images and the text, this chapter has explored the comics as they relate to the Negro spiritual woman and other more established stereotypes. One of the first self-titled comics to feature the character, *Before the Storm* (Pak) is important in the character's development as it follows Storm as a little girl, exploring her origin story, which, as we discussed, has not been done in the films to date.

Throughout the series, Ororo uses her powers for both her own and her adopted family's benefit, which is a subversive act that has not been present within the comic books thus far. However, even as a child, the comic book contains Ororo by showing her that her destiny, although important, lies in helping white men. Furthermore, for the young girl, Ororo, the Negro spiritual woman archetype is absolute. The audience is assured that the future Storm will not only "assist the white characters on their journeys," but she will put aside any journey of her own and prioritize theirs. While other X-Men characters also support the team in a similar way, it is arguable that Storm's African and African American ancestry is in opposition to the X-Men's mission in a way that the ancestries of white characters are not. In other words, because Storm is Black, working with the X-Men is repressive because she is supporting the very status quo that is oppressive to her as a Black woman.

Most interesting here is the Storm series written by Eric Jerome Dickey, a Black male writer. Within this series, Storm is just as much subjugated by her gender as she has been oppressed by her race in pervious works. The text links Storm's sexuality to womanhood, outright stating that she cannot become a woman until she has had sex with a man. There is no salvation for Storm within this text, as she is bound by the construction of patriarchal womanhood that is usually reserved for white women, which in the end oppresses non-ambiguously Black women. Although Storm is depicted as objectively more attractive and acceptable than the other Black women around her, this in itself is racist and sexist. This misogynoir[6] is meant to benefit Storm, while simultaneously oppressing all other Black women who are not blue eyed and white haired.

Dickey's use of Black female sexuality binds Storm's powers, containing her through them. Just as Linda Fite's reliance on white supremacists ideologies objectifies Storm's Blackness. This suggests that Black male–written works do not *necessarily* offer any more for freedom for Black women characters than stories by white writers.

5

Storm

•••••••••••••••••••••

The Films

The year is "the not-so-distant-future." The actual year is irrelevant as it could be any year in any time, and you could, in fact, be any person. In this time, it does not matter if you are Black or white, man or woman—there is no discrimination and racism has been eliminated. How, you ask, do you know this? Because they *told* you so. In fact, we all watch as you, Ethan Hawke, run around the screen scrubbing all evidence of your true self away, replacing it with DNA from another, more suitable white man. *Gattaca* (1997) is the future, and you can be assured that you will not be discriminated against because of your race or gender.

While it is "illegal to discriminate," you endure a new kind of xenophobia because you have not been genetically enhanced. Because of this, you are forced to live a secret life, always hiding who you are from the world, pretending to be something that you are not. "Genoism," is the new true name of bigotry in this world, and you, a white, male character played by Ethan Hawke, are the most tragic victim of it.

As you, generic white man who we all could be, fight against every form of injustice in the film, there is a notable absence. Something just there under the surface, but that you cannot quite put your finger on. But then it hits you. The thing that is missing is actual Black people, or really any marginalized group. While the film assures the viewer that racism has been eliminated, Black people are almost completely absent in this futuristic world—other than in secondary, non-important roles. The white imagination of a world without racism could not equally imagine a world where Black people exist as autonomous and vital to the future.

You have been subsumed by whiteness, your persecutions and the injustices that have been done to you generationally are ignored, thrown aside, and consumed by the greater inequality of whatever this new future world has created. But you have been entertained, and really, isn't that the point? So, nothing is amiss here.

Please, proceed with caution.

X-Men (2000)

We find ourselves back here again, with the longstanding Marvel comic book character Storm, who, it bears repeating, is arguably one of the most powerful mutants ever born. She is an Omega level mutant whose power is considered the greatest among mutants of her kind. We reiterate this because you would not ascertain that by watching the films alone. Once Queen of Wakanda, Storm possesses the ability to control all elements of the weather, both here on Earth and in extraterrestrial ecosystems. Despite all this power, however, in the comics Storm is mostly portrayed in scanty attire, with exposed breasts and skimpy thongs, as opposed to her male counterparts whose costumes cover their entire bodies. In the films, she is simply irrelevant.

The first film in the series, *X-Men* (Singer), introduces the mutants as they fight societal oppression. In the film, a U.S. Senator by the name of Robert Kelly wants to pass the "Mutant Registration Act" that would force mutants to divulge their identities and abilities to the world. Eventually Kelly is taken by Magneto, who imprisons him on the island of Genosha and turns him into a mutant. Magneto then kidnaps Rogue, who has the ability to absorb other mutants' powers, and plans to use her to power his machine, hoping to turn humans into mutants. After Kelly escapes, having become a mutant, he goes to the mutant school, where Xavier reads his mind to discover Magneto's plan to turn leaders at the world summit meeting at Ellis Island into mutants. The "good" mutants, such as the X-Men, must save the humans.

X-Men: Last Stand (2006). Storm is in a life and death battle when Logan calls out to her for help (Ratner).

Storm has very few lines throughout this film, and she is almost never seen in a position where she is not supporting the white male hierarchy. Storm's intersectionality, being a woman, Black, and a mutant, should at least inspire mistrust in her toward the broader society. Instead, she works tirelessly to ensure that the current racist, patriarchal society continues unquestioned. Circling back to Spike Lee, we must ask: "How is it that Black people have these powers, but they use them for the benefit of white people?" (Yale Bulletin & Calendar). This is an important question, as Storm's powers are so great that she could single-handedly empower whole groups of subjugated peoples if she cared to do so. Unfortunately, Storm is created in such a way that she only cares to protect the power structure as it currently exists.

Another site of contention for the character and fans comes in her appearance. Storm in the film series is played by a light-skinned Halle Berry. Storm from the comics, of course, has traditionally been depicted as a dark-skinned woman. As mentioned in the preface, her skin tone is important for her construction as a fully realized character. While Black and white people experience the world differently, it would be remiss not to copiously address the fact that light-skinned and dark-skinned people also often experience the world differently. In their article "Skin Complexion in the Twenty-First Century: The Impact of Colorism on African

American Women," authors Tayler J. Mathews and Glenn S. Johnson state that:

> There is an existing beauty standard characterized by skin complexion among African Americans that erodes the framework of cultural identity, inclusion, mobility, and social acceptance. This phenomenon has plagued the African American community since the period of slavery continues to hold true in today's society. Although it is well established that American society has intricate history in regards to race relations, an equally important matter has been given significant attention. The main characteristic that continues to separate the dominant groups from the non-dominant groups is skin color (Hunter, 2002; Azibo, 2014). Moreover, it "is apparent that colorist ideology based on not just skin pigmentation but all highly correlated physical traits hair texture, eye color and facial features (Cain, 2006:1)." (249)

Circling back to the discussion on Alexandra Shipp, light-skinned people with non-kinky hair and light eyes, particularly women, occupy social spaces differently than darker-skinned women and people. This is a site of contention within and outside of Black and other communities. However, while race is a determining factor in society, proximity to whiteness offers privilege that darker-skinned people do not experience. This is not just an invention of minority communities, as past research has "focused on cases in which interviewers were white and respondents were black and Latino, [and] after running ordinal logistic regression analyses on this data, [the researcher] found conclusively that 'African American and Latino respondents with the lightest skin are several times more likely to be seen by whites as intelligent compared with those with the darkest skin'" (Mathews and Johnson 250).

For Storm—from the films—whose physical features in the comics are conceptualized as not fitting any acceptable racial group, such as "Negroid, Caucasian, or Oriental" but are somehow considered a mixture of them all ("White hair. Blue eyes"), colorism affirms her position within whiteness, as her phenotype and other white-centered, typical features are manipulated by the white gaze to be acceptable to white society (Claremont 11). In this way, Storm, a Black woman with dark skin, has been manipulated to imitate white-centered forms of beauty that are not available to darker-skinned women. Beauty, as such, is connected to her light skin, which is then connected to her goodness.

Throughout the film, Storm uses her powers to keep humanity safe and to keep society functioning as it does. The mutants from the X-Men, who are considered the good guys, do not try to end poverty, sexism, or racism (other than prejudices against mutants). Indeed, these issues do not even seem to be acknowledged within the world any longer. Although they do not focus on these problems, they often fight other mutants who want to subvert the status quo, such as Magneto, who warns that "letting [humans have their way will] have [mutants] in chains with a number burned into [their] foreheads" (Singer, *X-Men*; 2000). Of course, the mutant/human struggle is an allegory for prejudice. However, even taking this into account, it can be argued that Storm wrongly sides with the humans, and this puts her in the unique position of having to not only choose between whiteness and Blackness, but to choose between her Blackness and her mutant powers.

At one point during this first film, Wolverine is wavering, as a mutant, between whether to side with the mutants such as Magneto or humans, who hate mutants. Wrestling with his decision, he asks Storm an important question. "Magneto's right. There is a war coming. Are you sure you're on the right side?" (Singer, *X-Men*; 2000). Without a thought, Storm answers: "At least I've chosen a side" (Singer, *X-Men*; 2000). If Wolverine, a white man who can in fact hide his mutant-ness, is written with the autonomy to decide his chosen path, why then is Storm, a Black woman who cannot hide either her mutant-ness or Blackness, used so passionately to silence all discussion of sovereignty? I offer a simple answer for this not-so-simple question: To bring up the question of autonomy for Storm is to force the reader to consider what actual autonomy looks like for this Black woman who, since a young child in that dark tomb, has been groomed to serve white men.

The audience should wonder, then, if this is the correct side, or simply the most convenient side for the society to place a Black woman character with so much power, so as not to be deemed a threat by that society. Wolverine can ask these questions; Storm must always appear to support the status quo. Although Storm is clearly a mutant (her white hair, changing eye color, and dark skin are a dead giveaway), having grown up as a Black woman within society, she would have been confronted with racial and gender prejudices. Likewise, it is not difficult to imagine that her mother and father would have at least introduced the concept of prejudices before they died. Many Black children learn these lessons from their parents from an early age. *Parent* magazine says that by around six years old discussing racism with children "becomes easier," because "hate [is] explicit" to children by this point (Arnold-Ratliff). Unsurprisingly, this article appears to be targeting white parents and children, whereas Black children may have already experienced or seen some form of racism by even this early age. Storm's parents died when she was young, however, it's not outside the realm of possibility that she would have had some understanding of race, and she also is *very* likely to have experienced it on her own throughout her life. However, the film and thus the white creators have not only ignored her backstory but have chosen to side with whiteness, as her powers are only used to benefit the white supremacist society lest they be uncontained, and thus considered dangerous.

In the end, however, within this film, this subjugation ensures that Storm, as a Black woman, continues to be marginalized through her supernatural powers, unable to free herself, as she instead must uphold the status quo, ignoring the oppression of the Black community, and Black women such as herself specifically. While it is hard to argue that she is constructed as any controlling image other than the magical Negro, she is not constructed as the Negro spiritual woman. Of course, that almost doesn't matter, as you could completely eliminate her from the entire film and it would not be impacted in any real way.

X2 (2003)

This second installment follows the X-Men again in a fight against politicians and the Mutant Registration Act. The main antagonist, William Stryker, is a military colonel and a scientist who has experimented on Wolverine, although the mutant does not fully remember what has happened to him. The humans want to find all the mutants in the world, and they steal Cerebro, Xavier's machine that can detect every person on the planet, especially so they can search out mutants for elimination. By the end, the X-Men have neutralized the threat of the government only to be forced to fight against Magneto again, as he reverses the aim of Cerebro, hoping to search out and eradicate all human beings instead.

As with the previous film, analyzing for controlling images becomes difficult because Storm has very little screen time. When she does appear on film, she is doing little more than supporting the oppression and silencing of other mutants. I suppose this is an effective tactic for ignoring race;

X2: X-Men United (2003.) Storm chastising a young mutant for stepping out of line (Singer).

simply take out racialized bodies. We see how well that works for *Gattaca*. But for this this reason, I offer broader readings of the film subject to race, gender, and other oppressions.

In an opening scene of the film, Storm is at a museum with the students of Xavier's school. One of the mutant children smiles at a little girl eating ice cream, but the girl sticks her tongue out at the boy, obviously being mean to him for no reason. The mutant child sticks his tongue back out at the girl—his tongue is lizard-like, dark and forked, split down the middle. The little girl is surprised and scared, and jumps, clearly having learned her lesson. Storm, seeing the interaction, chastises the young mutant, telling him that this was not the place to show himself.

Touching again on the connection between mutantism being a stand-in for injustice against minority and Black bodies, Professor X's school that indoctrinates students into a submissive role is representative of the United States' history of indoctrination of minority students, particular Indigenous Americans. In her article "Boarding School Abuses, Human Rights, and Reparations," Andrea Smith discusses the way that Native children were forcibly taken from their homes and indoctrinated into white ideology—in a similar way to the mutants of Xavier's school. Smith says:

> During the 19th century and into the 20th century American Indian
> children were forcibly abducted from their homes to attend Christian and
> US government run boarding schools as a matter of state policy. This system

had its beginnings in the 1600s, when John Elliott erected "praying towns" for American Indians, in which he separated them out from their communities to receive Christian "civilizing" instruction. However, colonist soon concluded that such practices should be targeted toward children because they believed adults were too set in their ways to become Christianized. Jesuit priest began to develop schools for Indian children along the Saint Louis River in the 1600s. (89)

Throughout U.S. history, minority groups have been targeted for elimination, not only through genocide but also through death of culture and assimilation. These schools cut off students' hair, punished Indigenous students for speaking their native languages, forced them to take new names and convert to Christianity, and beat and abused them into submission. Scholar Robert Trennert explains it further:

> During the latter part of the nineteenth century the Bureau of Indian Affairs made an intensive effort to assimilate the Indian into American society. One important aspect of the government's acculturation program was Indian education. By means of reservation day schools, reservation boarding schools, and off-reservation industrial schools, the federal government attempted to obliterate the cultural heritage of Indian youths and replace it with the values of Anglo-American society. One of the more notable aspects of this program was the removal of young Indian women from their tribal homes to government schools in an effort to transform them into a government version of the ideal American. (271)

The point was to create a permanent subordinate class of nonwhite, Native people. Knowing that it would be easier to indoctrinate large groups rather than completely wipe them out, the U.S. government systematically worked to destabilize the families of differing minority groups. They created schools in which the education was tailored to the elimination of these children's cultures. This type of corrupted education did not only happen to Indigenous children.

As a Black child growing up in Hopkinsville, Kentucky, I knew my grandmother had not gone past elementary school and could not read, despite her insisting that we all get educations. I also knew that my grandmother likely had a photographic memory, as she had a little black book in which she had dozens and dozens of numbers, from church members to utility companies and friends and family members, written in what my grandmother herself often joked was "chicken scratch." None of the numbers in the book had names attached to them, as she could not spell, and yet she always knew whose number belonged to whom. She simply remembered. Why, then, did my grandmother not finish school? What I did not know growing up, but learned as an adult, was that during my grandmother's time in that region, there was no school for Black children beyond that point. There was in effect a forced illiteracy for Black people similar to that of the slavery era. Not educating children has the same impact as cultural indoctrination. It silences, forcing people into submission through lack of knowledge and education.

This in effect is what Xavier does to mutant children in his school. This is what Marisol fears so badly, locked away in Xavier's schoolhouse that is eerily reminiscent of the Indigenous indoctrination camps.

Furthermore, Storm forcing the mutant child to be more responsible than the human one relies completely on this same assimilation ideology, because it instills the idea that the most oppressed groups must behave in ways that assuage the oppressors—forcing compliance that the dominant group themselves never have to abide. While there is some debate on whether Professor X (Xavier) and Magneto are based on Martin Luther King and Malcolm X, respectively, these characters are often expected to respond passively toward violence inflicted against them in a way similar to how Black and other minority groups are expected to behave within society. Structuring this mutant society in this way alone is problematic, as it not only upholds the white-created illusion of MLK's passiveness (to refute the illusion, see his critique of "white moderates" in "Letter from a Birmingham Jail," chapter 4) but it also supports the fantasy of constructed oppression to silence real oppression against real people.

In 2019, in response to Judge Tammy Kemp hugging convicted murderer Amber Guyger, who is white and killed an unarmed Black man, Botham Jean, Reis Thebault wrote for the *Washington Post*, "Some praised it as a rare moment of compassion in a cold criminal justice system, while others derided it as a grave ethical breach and yet another example of how white defendants are treated better than defendants of color." In response to the backlash, the judge told the Associated Press that "following [her] own convictions, [she] could not refuse that woman a hug. [She] would not. And [she doesn't] understand the anger." The anger is rooted in the understanding that there is a two-tier justice system that privileges whiteness. Studies show that within the justice system Black people rarely get that same compassion. Not only this, but research suggests that when confronted with evidence that racial disparities in the justice system exist, people are more like to support those disparities, as scholars Rebecca C. Hetey and Jennifer L. Eberhardt outline clearly in the abstract of their article, "The Numbers Don't Speak for Themselves: Racial Disparities and the Persistence of Inequality in the Criminal Justice System":

> Many scholars and activists assume the public would be motivated to fight
> inequality if only they knew the full extent of existing disparities. Ironically,
> exposure to extreme disparities can cause people to become more, not less,
> supportive of the very policies that create those disparities (Hetey & Eberhardt,
> 2014). Here, we focus on the criminal justice system—policing and incarceration in particular. We argue that bringing to mind racial disparities in this
> domain can trigger fear and stereotypic associations linking Black people
> with crime. Therefore, rather than extending an invitation to reexamine the
> criminal justice system, the statistics about disparities may instead provide an
> opportunity to justify and rationalize the disparities found within that
> system. With the goals of spurring future research and mitigating this
> paradoxical and unintended effect, we propose three potential strategies for
> more effectively presenting information about racial disparities: (a) offer
> context, (b) challenge associations, and (c) highlight institutions. (183)

In other words, when given the opportunity, the American public often supports using the justice system in this country to over-police and imprison Black and other racial minorities intentionally. So, with this, we can also understand that Black people are less likely to walk away with a ten-year sentence for murder and/or a hug from the judge to assuage our guilt. But outside of not getting compassion, Black people are too often expected to give it to white people despite the harm that has systemically been committed against them since the formation of this country. The judge here admits that she has never hugged a defendant before and yet somehow hugging a white woman who murdered a Black man is where she finds it most beneficial to start. This sets up the dynamic that white people's violence against Black bodies is something that can be loved away, with the right compassion and attitude on the part of Black people. It is the stagnant position in which Storm finds herself—stuck supporting, comforting, and serving white people with little of this support and comfort given in return. Because she is also constructed as the strong Black woman, and the mammy so that her submission to whiteness is absolute.

A good Black person, like Storm, forgives whiteness for its terrorism against Black bodies, while bad minorities, like Marisol, do not. More importantly, this construct makes passivity for minorities more noble and righteous. Conversely, anyone who is not willingly passive when faced with subjugation must be weeded out. This is reiterated later at the museum; when other teen mutants are bullied by stereotypical teen thugs, they choose to strike back with their powers, but the lesson on passivity is placed at the forefront. Xavier freezes everyone human in the building to teach the mutant children humility, the lesson that he believes all mutants must learn, even in the face of adversity.

Now one could reasonably argue that "with great power comes great reasonability," as Xavier does later in the series. While teaching a class at the school, the mutant leader tells other young mutants that "When an individual acquires great power, the use or misuse of that power is everything. Will it be for the greater good? Or will it be used for the personal or destructive ends? This is the question we must all ask ourselves." The problem, of course, is that the true power lies in the structural system that seeks to oppress mutants and not in the individual mutants themselves. It lies in the ignored oppression of Black and other marginalized groups that the films refuse to recognize.

There is always someone bigger and more dangerous, and each of those individuals must act responsibly and compassionately in their dealings with others. The girl sticking her tongue out at the little boy, and his response in kind although his tongue is bigger and more dangerous in appearance, is one example. If the young girl had never done the first action, the second action would never have happened. But the burden of peace cannot lie in the hands of those who are least likely to be able to protect themselves at the hands of unparalleled military force. Mutants (and by extension Black people) cannot be burdened with both protecting and fighting against a human (and white) supremacist power structure that does nothing but want them dead or at least neutralized. It is an unreasonable ideology that only works to protect the status quo: white people.

Storm consistently makes herself unavailable, literally excusing herself when seemingly more important people are around. At one point she removes herself from the budding relationship between Wolverine and Jean Gray. While this is a relatively minor moment, it becomes more and more

obvious that the creators clearly have no use for her other than quick one-
liners and supporting roles. Storm simply has no real significance other than
to "make it rain" at the times in the film when her power is needed, but her
Blackness would be an inconvenience.

Because the film clearly wants to avoid the topic of race, racism, and other
oppressions that are not mutantphobia, Storm's Black presence alone upsets
the storyline's need to center oppression that is not anti-Blackness. While
the character's skin is not dark, her racial background visibly disrupts the
film's central premise: that the most oppressed group in this country are
mutants. The question left to the preceptive viewer is simple: If Storm isn't
oppressed by racism as well as mutantism, why is she invisible? The real problem with the treatment of Storm in this film is that no one seems to actually "see" her; we only see the service that she can provide through her
powers.

Films rely on a need for the suspension of disbelief. In *An Introduction
to Film Studies*, Jill Nelmes explains it this way:

> The "illusory reality" of mainstream cinema is created for us by a number
> of devices, involving the use of camera, microphone and lighting. These
> devices are not fixed—a "correct" way of recording the truth—but conven-
> tions developed over a hundred years of cinema. These are ingrained in us
> as viewers—and we can feel disturbed or cheated if these conventions are
> broken. If we are "duped" by this—we are willingly duped. We participate in
> this process of suspension of disbelief as a price for the pleasures we get from
> film viewing—including that of "surviving." (89)

Film creators work hard not to break the fourth wall[1] unintentionally, to
keep the trust of the viewer. Given too much screen time, Storm's Black body
becomes the point of tension in the film, as a racialized person in this society. Any viewer with an understanding of the history of racial politics in
this country will find themselves asking logical questions that the film does
not want to answer. The main inquiry, of course, would be, "But what about
racism? Or sexism?"

In the film, Storm has a budding relationship with Nightcrawler, a fellow mutant of color who cannot hide his mutant-ness, even more than
Storm. The blue mutant tells her that he pities humans because many of
them will not know anything beyond their own two eyes. Storm responds

by saying that she gave up on "pity" long ago. Never one to dismantle the patriarchy, the creators insist Nightcrawler tell her that she is too pretty to be angry. Instead of addressing the insult that somehow her beauty should make her calmer and mild mannered, she responds to the other insulting part of his statement, telling him that "sometimes anger can help you survive" (Singer, $X2$). He has the last word, however, advising her that she does not have enough faith.

There is so much to unpack here, it's difficult to know where to start. On the one hand, Nightcrawler, an oppressed man, is using his privilege in a patriarchal system to silence a Black woman, a fellow mutant. Like Storm, he is not white and is clearly a mutant. While it's unacceptable to use mutantism (or aliens, robots, and so on) as a replacement for anti-Blackness and other racism, we cannot ignore that this is the result, whether by the creator's intention or not. When Nightcrawler tells Storm that she is too beautiful to be angry, he is suggesting that her ideas and critical understanding of the world are secondary to her looks and attractiveness to the opposite sex. It is a way to shut her down, for the contentment of the men around her.

The scene is, in effect, a site of double oppression for Storm. In her article "Multiple Jeopardy, Multiple Consciousness: The Context of a Black Feminist Ideology," Deborah K. King states that:

> For [Black women], the notion of double jeopardy is not a new one. Near the end of the nineteenth century, Anna Julia Cooper, who was born a slave and later became an educator and earned a Ph.D., often spoke and wrote of the double enslavement of black women and of our being "confronted by both a woman question and a race problem." [. . .] The dual and systemic discriminations of racism and sexism remain pervasive, and, for many, class inequality compounds those oppressions. (42)

Whereas Storm and Nightcrawler should share an understanding and unity, he uses his privilege as male to silence her concerns, as she has used hers to silence others previously. He positions her as "good" due to her beauty and connects that goodness to accepting the position of peacemaker for those who seek to do her harm. In pushing back against this, Storm would have been forced to have the dual conversation of the "double enslavement of black women" and further put herself in the position of appearing unreasonable.

Worse still is that Nightcrawler uses "faith" to challenge Storm's womanhood, suggesting that being angry contrasts with who she appears to be on the outside (beautiful), and that this is not godly. Historically womanhood has been represented by white women, as scholar Isis Settles states:

> Within the United States, socio-historical factors have created differences in the gender-role norms typically held for Black and White women. Many of these differences grew out of the *cult of true womanhood* (Perkins, 1983; Welter, 1966), a notion of womanhood that emerged for White (middle-class) women in the mid-1800s. This ideal emphasized modesty, purity, and domesticity for White women and identified wife and mother as their primary and most important roles. Historically, Black women were viewed in contrast to this norm for middle-class White women. Black women were not seen as "true" women, but rather as animalistic and hypersexed, which was then used to justify their enslavement and rape (Collins, 2000; West, 2004). There is evidence that these historical ideals persist in the stereotypes of Black and White women [even today]. (455)

The threat that Storm's womanhood and faith is in jeopardy is meant to keep her in line, silence her, and make her behave as an acceptable white woman would. This is a precarious position for Storm, repeating Cheryl Lynn's point that after all, Storm is what "all Black women want, or are told we should want by the media." She cannot simply be a Black woman in this moment. She cannot simply be a mutant in this moment. She must also smile and be amendable for the man to feel comfortable with her. In other words, the soon-to-be leader of the X-Men must make herself "smaller" for the man she met only hours before.

The Christianity suggested in Nightcrawler using "faith" in this moment is a cheap shot. While in the comics Nightcrawler's religion is important to him, it is barely used in the film at all—only to silence Storm. Black women and Christianity have a long history. It has been used to justify the oppression of Black bodies (for instance, the Curse of Cain, which posits that after Cain killed his brother Abel and was banished by God, Cain mated with apes and created Black people). The problem of course is that Christianity's ideal of forgiveness is too often forced on the oppressed. Oppressors, on the other hand, have righteous anger and laws on their side. Black people are expected to forgive injustice against them because Christ would have done so. But white people's anger and violence against Black people is justified (e.g., Curse of Cain) and supported by laws and the white supremacist patriarchy in ways that are never afforded to Black people. Moreover, the promise of a happy and fruitful afterlife in heaven is the reward for Black people of faith if they toe the line. This encompasses the threat against a nonconforming Storm.

On the flip side, what Storm does say does not work either. She claims that she gave up on pity long ago, suggesting that she is hardened to humanity because of their treatment of mutants—except there is absolutely no evidence of this in either this film or any others. If she has truly given up on human beings, then why does not use her powers against them when they are clearly so harmful for her mutant community, her Black community, and her community of fellow women of all racial backgrounds?

This speaks to the fact that she is only useful for whiteness when she is working to uphold the power structure as it exists. Clearly Storm's power is a threat, and the screen is seemingly bursting with the tension around what is not being addressed. Instead, Storm makes herself small, running off-screen at the slightest hint of race or gendered discourse. She must always be seen upholding the status quo, lest her ability to potentially destroy the world breaks through the fourth wall.

X-Men: The Last Stand (2006)

This film is Jean Grey. Grey, a mutant whose telepathic abilities are continuously unstable to the point of threatening total human annihilation, comes back from death, changed and even more unstable than she has been in previous films. Having repressed Jean's "dark" side as a child, Xavier now explains that after her death her evil side is free. The reincarnated Jean Gray has little in common with the old Jean Gray and she soon kills Xavier and aligns with Magneto to destroy humanity. In the final battle, many mutants are killed, Magneto is injected with anti-mutant serum, effectively turning him human, and Jean is killed again, this time by Logan.

Here is where I must admit that Jean Gray is my least favorite mutant. As a kid I always felt she was whiny in a way that never satisfied my need for a badass woman character that got shit done, and who spoke to me in a representational way. As an adult, I feel that she does not satisfy these same needs. But now I have the language to understand why, in a way that I did not as a child. To put it simply and to bring back my analysis of the Karen, I must say that Jean Gray is the ultimate Karen.

While I dislike Jean Gray, I'm obsessed with critical analysis of the Karen, often watching the viral videos that have permeated our cultural understanding of the way white womanhood is constructed in society. From my cellphone, I watch as white people, very often women, call the police on Black people and other racial minorities for simply existing in nonwhite skin. What we all have learned by watching these videos is that many white women all over the country are toxic for Black and marginalized people.

Karens cause harm to the people around them while playing victim. This is Jean Gray. In *Last Stand* (Ratner), Jean's personal anguish becomes a death sentence for countless people. To use a rather appropriate analogy, she has a direct line to the police and a short temper, and the mutants that die due to her actions are representative of the Black people that may die as soon as Karen dials 911 to report whatever pisses her off in that moment. The analogy may not be completely sound, as Gray does not have complete control over her actions, but I could similarly argue—having watched more Karen videos than I care to admit—that most Karens do not in fact have control over their actions. And although they all have the opportunity to take themselves out of the situation, they almost never do. In Jean's case, she has moments of clarity, gaining full control again, even begging Logan to kill her. From the moment that she returns, she knows something is wrong, but she does not do anything about it. The viewer must ask, though: Why, if Jean has these moments of clarity, does she not remove herself from the situation? Or, why not use her enormous power to simply destroy herself, since she wants this anyway? I am sure there are a lot of reasons for why neither of these are done but all of them will be constructed. The simplest reason is that she is written by, for, and about white people. Thus, her actions are viewed sympathetically by the audience, in the same way that people sympathize and defend racists Karens who go viral.

But this is not the Jean Gray book, thank God. This is the book on Storm.

Here is the problem. In *Last Stand*, Storm spends so much time mammying the students at the school she barely has any agency of her own. As in the previous films, she has no central storyline. There is just not a lot to say about her in this film that has not already been said, and I suppose that itself is saying a lot about how Storm is constructed as a character—and what her creators think of her. She has no growth. No—as far as we

X-Men: Last Stand (2006). Storm's powers on full display until Xavier makes her apologize for being sad (Ratner).

know—aspirations, and she is never in a scene with other Black people. This film would never pass the racial Bechdel test,[2] which would ask whether a character ever interacts with another nonwhite character—but this is because there are hardly any other Black people in the entire X-Men world. She is seemingly the lone, valuable Black character in the X-Men Universe. Black and other minority groups are on the periphery if they are there at all. There are precious few Black students at the school, so either Black people are less likely to become mutants, or the school is less likely to take in Black students. Take your pick, but neither of these is acceptable. Like the world of *Gattaca*, this world is devoid of Black people, and you, the viewer, are expected to believe that this is because they have eliminated racism in favor of mutant bigotry. But what we all understand by now is that racism is inherent in Hollywood's avoidance of racial issues and, as in *Last Stand*, in even depicting Black people as existing at all.

There is an interesting moment in the film that could signal to race, however. Mystic, a mutant that can shape-shift into any creature she wishes, has been taken captive and is being interrogated. The interrogator constantly refers to her as "Raven," a name given to her by the humans. In response, Mystic tells the man that she refuses to answer to her "slave name." Likewise, earlier in the series, when Nightcrawler finds out what Mystic's mutant powers are, he asks her why she doesn't just stay in human form to protect herself. Mystic is appalled at this question, scolding him that she should not have to do that to be accepted. Being a mutant and a blue woman (a "woman of color," so to speak), Mystic is used as a stand-in to represent race. And she is not wrong in either of these moments. Mystic, unlike Storm, can express these feelings because her alter self is a white woman, and white women do not threaten the racial hierarchy. In Mystic's statement patriarchy and white supremacy are not exposed at all, so the world is safe.

Not only does Storm not say anything approaching this, but also we cannot imagine the passive-presenting Halle Berry/Storm saying this at all. The idea that mutant-ness is a stand in for racism is exactly the problem for this reason. It claims to be a way to talk about racism and injustice without actually talking about it, but in reality, it is simply a way to avoid discussions on race altogether. Mystic, being a fictional character, is fun to fantasize and write about without the actual threat of systemic change to the status quo in real life. Mystic and Magneto could end anti-mutant bigotry by the end of this film, and racism would remain the same, both in the film and in reality.

X-Men: Days of Future Past (2014)

Post a human-mutant war, the world is in disarray, and most of the world has been decimated. Mutants have been murdered or rounded up and the X-Men seek to correct the timeline, sending Logan into the past to stop

X-Men: Days of Future Past (2014). Storm's anticlimactic death (Singer).

Mystic from killing a top official, which has caused the chain of events that put them on the path to where they are now.

Yet again, Storm has precious few minutes on the screen, and she is killed rather anticlimactically, although the audience knows that she will likely be resurrected. There is, finally, a Black male X-Man in a speaking position (Bishop, played by actor Omar Sy), but his role is small and he suffers the same fate as Storm, dying with the promise of coming back, as he did so at the beginning of the film as well. While Storm has seemingly even less screen time in this film than the previous ones, that does not mean there is nothing to say about race, gender, and controlling images.

Once Logan is sent back in time, he is tasked with getting the past versions of Magneto and Xavier to join him in the mission of stopping Mystic from killing the official. The past version of Xavier is a mess, having lost most of his students to the war, and he has become an addict, shooting up drugs more than Hank (Nicholas Hoult) thinks is acceptable. Xavier eventually agrees to help, and the group (Logan, Xavier, and Hank) set out to free Magneto from imprisonment in the concrete-enforced substructures of the Pentagon. He is there for having killed President Kennedy.

After getting him out, the group is stopped by armed guards who fire on them without warning. To protect them from danger, Magneto begins to use his powers to stop them. Xavier does not allow this, instead having another mutant who possesses the speed of light peacefully end the attack.

The moment is an exercise in frustration for anyone even reasonably familiar with the series. Xavier's constant need to keep mutants from protecting themselves from humans is at once infuriating and odd. Even when faced with danger, Xavier seems to believe that mutants are charged with protecting humans, as if they are themselves expendable, and it is their duty to suffer for them. If, again, mutants are an allegory for race, then this makes sense. Black people's lives are not valued in the same way as whites, and we are often expected to defend whites even when they seek to harm us. We are their real-life magical Negros.

Like racism, Xavier's ideologies have long-term impacts. We have seen Storm chastise mutant children, putting them in their place when they step out of line. In a scene in *Last Stand* (Ratner), Rogue, Wolverine, and two other mutants are held at gunpoint by police officers and when one of the mutants uses his powers, again, to protect them, Rogue uses hers against the mutant instead of the police who have just shot Logan—one of her best friends—in the head. The message for the mutants, and for the viewer, is clear. The status quo must be upheld at all times, even and especially when it is against those with power against a marginalized group. At this point, this X-Men film series appears to be little more than American, racial propaganda.

When Xavier and Magneto discuss Mystic's decision to kill a man, Xavier refuses to accept her decision as autonomous because "the girl [he] raised" would never do that (Singer, *Days of Future Past*). Xavier and Mystic are about the same age; he met her when she was starving and broke into his parent's home for food; and as a child, he offered to feed her. This assertion that he "raised her" is as absurd as it is sexist. Xavier has infantilized Mystic to the point that he barely even sees her as an adult. He has created an entire narrative around having saved and protected her as a child, while conveniently forgetting that she is an autonomous adult making autonomous decisions, just as he is.

If Jean Gray is the ultimate Karen, Xavier is the perfect analogy for male whiteness. He is arrogant, angry, and spends too much of the film whining about not wanting to feel the pain of others. Throughout the series, Xavier spends an exorbitant amount of time trying to teach others how to use their powers, often taking a moral stance around when and how they use them. Yet, when it is time, he cannot find the same energy to do it for himself.

To fully address injustice in a meaningful way is to address the lived experiences of mutants (Black people), and too often white creators are unwilling to do the mental work that it would require. It would also mean addressing that mutantism, racism, sexism, and other oppressions would be a driving force in characters' lives. More importantly, it would mean not using anti-mutant bigotry as a replacement for racism and other injustices against minority peoples.

Putting this into context, addressing racial injustice is to admit that white supremacy is a functioning part of society; that it is systemic, and must be dismantled. White supremacy and patriarchy, however, cannot admit to its unearned, unacknowledged privilege, despite mounds of evidence, because to admit privilege is to move one step closer to eliminating hook's white, supremacist, capitalist, patriarchy. Xavier, however, exists as a perpetual oppressor within the series—he supports the status quo and is supported by it.

X-Men: Apocalypse (2016)

It is refreshing, in a way, to have a storyline in which Storm is actually featured in the beginning. Likewise, Africa being centered in the film is particularly worth noting, as research shows that Africa is often still depicted in films as dangerous and untouched by civilization, the "dark continent." This is no different in *X-Men: Apocalypse* (Singer) because it shows the continent to be a place of unstable, corrupt people, who are desolate and cannot take care of themselves. This is the same as the depiction of Africa from the X-Men comics. Unfortunately, however, Storm's role proves as insignificant as in the previous films; pretty much her entire part could be removed without impacting the storyline, like every other film in this series. But, for the sake of argument, let's examine the evidence. Here is Marvel's write-up of the film:

> Upon awakening after thousands of years, Apocalypse is disillusioned with the world as he finds it and recruits a team of powerful mutants, including a disheartened Magneto (Michael Fassbender), to cleanse mankind and create a new world order, over which he will reign. As the fate of the Earth hangs in the balance, Raven (Jennifer Lawrence) with the help of Professor X (James McAvoy) must lead a team of young X-Men to stop their greatest nemesis and save mankind from complete destruction. (Marvel.com)

Notice how many of the other major mutants are mentioned? Storm is not only left out, but from reading this, you would not even know that she appears in this film at all. This is possibly because of bigotry of the writer, or, more likely, Storm is simply not relevant despite the film being based in Africa, Storm's homeland, and her being the first mutant Apocalypse inducts.

One of the refreshing things about this film that does not exists in the others is somewhat of an origin story for Storm. Comic book fans of the character will not be satisfied, but those who do not read comics and crave more of Storm will be pleasantly surprised. We learn that Storm is destitute and must steal for her survival, but even so, she takes in some of the other impoverished children, possibly offering them a place of refuge from homelessness, though this is not made clear. When Storm brings Apocalypse home after he saves her life, he asks her why she "enslaves herself," and gives her a gift, making her more powerful, turning her hair white.

X-Men: Apocalypse (2016). Apocalypse making Storm "stronger," in the process making her hair whiter, and in doing so stripping more autonomy from the character because yet again a man has control over her powers (Ratner).

This contradicts most of the comics, but the storyline offers Storm the humanity that the previous films have not.

Likewise, the introduction of the idea that Storm has enslaved herself is sound, but flawed. First, it is somewhat true. Storm willingly submits to Xavier and the X-Men for no real reason that makes sense outside of white supremacy and the patriarchy. However, the assertion that she has "enslaved herself" ignores the reality of Storm's life. As a poor, semi-immigrant, Black woman, she has not chosen her position; she has been forced into a position that oppresses her.

This leads to a second point: Apocalypse's suggestion is that whatever oppression that Storm is experiencing is happening due to her own actions. Having examined the previous films with this character, this misstatement is not surprising. Storm has essentially been gaslit throughout the entire film series; any concerns or justified anger she might have are downplayed. Gaslighting—a term made popular by the 1944 film *Gaslight*, about a husband who works to drive his wife insane by controlling her reality—is psychological manipulation of people that forces them to question their own sanity. When it comes to race, Angelique M. Davis and Rose Ernst state that:

> Racial gaslighting offers a way to understand how white supremacy is
> sustained over time. We define racial gaslighting as the political, social,

economic and cultural process that perpetuates and normalizes a white supremacist reality through pathologizing those who resist. Just as racial formation rests on the creation of racial projects, racial gaslighting, as a process, relies on the production of particular narratives. (763)

At every opportunity, the creators of the X-Men series have ignored any chance to address race, leaving the topic completely unexplored. Instead, the series has used mutant-ness as a stand-in for racism, denying that racism is a functioning part of the society for Storm, one of the only Black people to appear in the films, and in most cases throughout the series. When racism is apparent, they dismiss it as something else entirely, maintaining the illusion that in fact racism is not the problem at all, but instead it's one individual's problem, and it is not the system that enables racism and sexism.

In the film, there are two minority women, and both align with Apocalypse, the bad guy. This is not necessarily a problem. The other characters having gaslit the Black woman throughout the series suggest that the women may be looking for autonomy that is not present within the X-Men group. Apocalypse offers them the world, with few strings attached. While Apocalypse expects loyalty, he does not seek to control the women as Xavier does. He also does not harbor any illusions around what he's done for them, as Xavier does when he infantilizes and gaslights the women around him.

By the end of the film, it becomes clear that Xavier has spent a long time trying to get his X-Men to suppress their powers to make human beings feel safer, and that it has become detrimental to the individuals and the group. None of the X-Men are prepared to fight such a formidable enemy as Apocalypse, and they flounder, all of them nearly dying in the process. In the final battle scene, the entire group of X-Men, all their powers combined, cannot defeat Apocalypse. However, it is the Dark Phoenix, the evil inside Jean Gray, that saves them all. Gray is forced to ignore Xavier's teaching and use her full strength, not holding back, not shrinking a part of herself to make him feel comfortable.

Professor X's (Xavier's) way is through control and manipulation. It is oppressive for the Black and women characters that have fewer ways to find agency within the racist, patriarchal system. If, however, he would put at least as much trust in the mutants with whom he has been charged as he does in human beings that he has never met, then they would have the tools they need to defeat Apocalypse. Of course, he doesn't until he is forced to do so.

Hank claims that Xavier "thinks the best of people. He has faith" (Singer, *X-Men: Apocalypse*). The faith of the leader of the X-Men, however, is based solely on the protection and devotion to humanity, at the expense of the lives of mutants.

X-Men: Dark Phoenix (2019)

Jean Gray. Is there anything else to say? This is likely the worst film in the series, but we will let the critics speak on that. This film follows Jean Gray, the problem child, now that the rest of the world has come to accept mutants. In fact, mutant-human relations are such that they collaborate on missions to continue saving the planet. Humans finally see the potential of "superheroes" among the mutants; this excites Xavier, as he relishes having "created a world where children can have pride" in themselves no matter who they are (Kinberg, *Dark Phoenix*). Gray and the other mutants go into space to save astronauts when she is accosted by an otherworldly lifeform that merges with her, making her the most powerful mutant on the planet.

Storm has more screen time than she has had in some of the previous films, but still this film is for and about Jean Gray and thus there is little more character development of Storm than there has been since the first film in 2000, nineteen years before. The audience learns nothing new about Storm; she is constructed to uphold the status quo as she has in the past. It's arguably worse in *Dark Phoenix*. At one point, the young students at the school decide to have a party and Cyclops needs to fill Jean Gray's cup, so he walks up to Storm and demands one thing: "Ice." On command, the Black woman activates her powers to fill Jean Gray's cup with ice. And just like that, Storm, one of the most powerful mutants on the planet, is relegated to the role of an ice making machine, nothing more.

This might be seen as a moment of humiliation for the character, but the truth is that there have been many of those moments for Storm throughout the series (her ridiculous one-liner in the first film comes to mind: "Do you know what happens to a toad when it's hit by lightning? The same thing that happens to everything else"). But this is only symptomatic of the larger picture, which is that the white creators simply do not know what to do with Storm. As a mutant, they recognize that she must work to support Xavier, but as a Black woman they do not comprehend that this does not work for her in the same way as it does for, say, Jean Gray. While the comics did this

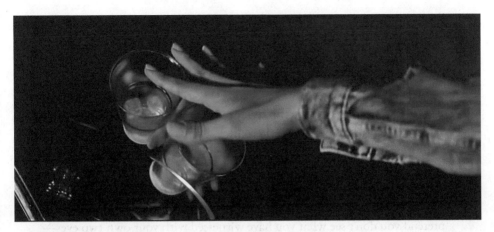

X-Men: Dark Phoenix (2019). Storm, the Icemaker (Kinberg).

to varying degrees, the films' creators have no other way to construct her, no understanding of who she is, and seemingly have never read the comics in their lives. There is so much more material in the comics because there is simply so much more space in the pages for Storm to fill. But also, the films are lacking because the construction of race in Hollywood functions so that fundamentalist ideologies of white patriarchy are upheld absolutely, without interrogation.

Almost none of the constructed stereotypes for Black women are present for Storm in this film because she is not written as germane to the script. Like almost all the X-Men films featuring Storm, from 2000 to today (with the arguable exception of *Apocalypse* [Singer, 2016]), she just is not relevant at all, even and especially when she is the leader of the group. The films effectively ignore her race, her gender, and her sexuality, successfully binding her completely. She is useless, invisible.

Of course, it is possible to have a discussion around whiteness within this film, as the absence of Blackness speaks to the creator's intention. But that discussion has already been done on multiple levels in this book. The point, of course, is that there is literally nothing new for the character and she has had no character growth for over *six* films and nearly *twenty* years. Let that sink in. While the conversation on race has grown on the national stage in that twenty-year time frame, Hollywood still cannot imagine a Black woman superhero that is not bound to the chains of the white supremacist patriarchy. Tara Thornton would be ashamed, even as the creators of True Blood would be proud.

Conclusion

You made it into the present. The actual year is 2023, and you are yourself, real, not constructed. Discrimination—as you have watched it unfold over about the last twenty years in this chapter—is still very much alive and well and being transmitted to you through your television, theater, and computer screens, even through the superhero films that you enjoy. And the comic books you read. Genoism is not real. It never was. But racism, sexism, and other oppressions definitely are. Black people are still almost completely absent on film in this present world—other than in secondary, non-important roles. The white imagination that lied to you now wants you to pretend you don't see what you have witnessed with your own two eyes—or more accurately, they want you to ignore what is not represented, and what you have not been shown.

But you will not do that any longer. You are smarter and wiser than they give you credit.

The Storm of the comics is nowhere in this film franchise. This is a great disservice to the characters and the fans. Furthermore, much as we hate to admit, it has become clear that the Storm of Hollywood is more oppressed than the one in the comics. This, of course, is not a get-out-of-jail-free card for the comics, as the previous chapter shows. Storm's supernatural powers, in both the comics and films, not only do not upset the racial and gender hierarchy, but they forge a constant battle among her race, gender, and sexuality, causing an inner conflict where she is forced to choose among these identities. In fact, it's hard to reconcile why a Black woman within this society would support the status quo, ensuring that humans, who are against mutants, are protected—especially as she is ignored, and her labor is used to support white supremacy.

In the comics, Storm is given the space to find love, fight for her Black community, and make decisions for the betterment of the group in a way that is almost unimaginable for the film version of Storm.

Let me take this moment to be very honest. I took on the challenge of re-watching these films because I had, if not relatively fond memories, at least not terrible ones of the film version of Storm's character. Memories are false gods, however. Like nostalgia, they keep us relegated to a time and place built on emotions that are, more often than not, compartmentalized within our minds, often recollecting things that are not true or that never happened to maintain a sense of peace within one's mind. My memories deceived me, and it's likely yours have deceived you as well. Neither of us should make the mistake of confusing nostalgia with reality.

As long as society keeps pretending that racism, sexism, classism, homophobia, and so on do not matter, individuals will continue to ignore the issues that permeate society simply because it does not impact them in any way. This willful ignorance allows one to ignore glaring disparities while maintaining that minorities are the true problem in society, feminism is ruining the world, poor people should just work harder, and "the gays" are trying to erode American families, instead of facing real injustices head-on for the betterment of all people. Refusing to acknowledge and ultimately examine the fallacies of race and gender within our society helps no one. But it hurts everyone who is not in the dominant position; or some variation of white, male, and/or privileged.

One of the most fascinating differences between the film and the comics is Storm's eyes. While her eyes turn black in the comics to alert the reader that she is out of control and needs to be contained, in the films her eyes are white, the symbol that white people have historically used to represent purity, suggesting to the viewer that she is already worthy to be an American superhero. Storm's eyes become white to signal to white people that she is virtuous, good, and completely contained. Other than this, it quickly becomes redundant and ultimately useless to do an analysis on the character in relation to controlling images, as Storm is barely present in any the films. Is she a mammy because she is charged with taking care of the white students and indoctrinating them with mutant ideologies? Is she a magical Negro because she only uses her powers for the greater purpose of the white society, to her own detriment? Of course, she is all of these things—but little more, just as she existed in the exact same way in every single film from 2000 to 2019. Over nearly a twenty-year time fame she has changed very little, if at all. She got younger and possibly lighter. But neither of these things adds to her character development. And this is the problem: Storm's character is not given the space or the opportunity to grow into anything productive or useful for the community at large.

This leaves the final stereotype, the Negro spiritual woman, to consider. Is Storm the NSW within the film versions of the X-Men franchise? Well, let's examine one of the central arguments of this book: "The Negro spiritual woman image should be distinguished from its predecessor, the magical Negro, because they differ in three important factors: submissiveness, mysteriousness, and sexuality. Although the magical Negro trope can include the first two, it is the third aspect that separates the NSW from the MN, its antecedent. As constructs, both images work to affirm society's ideology and current structure, but only the Negro spiritual woman image uses the sexuality of Black women to reinforce their current social status" (chapter 2).

Storm is submissive. She seems to occupy no space within the films other than to be submissive to the main characters. But as I have already said, she is mammied within these films. Is, then, she mysterious and does she have power? Yes, she is the magical Negro. That leaves us with the sexuality. Viewers would be hard-pressed to find any moment where Storm's sexuality is apparent in these films. Not even when Nightcrawler is flirting with her does she acknowledge it in any significant way. If she had been a male character, the viewer could imagine that she had somehow become a eunuch down in those tunnels in Africa—that is, if the films had even bothered to give her a storyline that puts her front and center in any way, or even a backstory to that puts her in tunnel for any reason. But they do not. It's true that doing so would disrupt the racial hierarchy in a way that Hollywood finds uncomfortable. But there's more than this, is there not?

"Re-Framing Hottentot: Liberating Black Female Sexuality from the Mammy/Hottentot Bind" by Shaweta Nanda states:

> The dominant representations of Black womanhood were centered on their bodies. Numerous myths were circulated about them in the form of "jokes" and "stereotypes" which then served to popularize and normalize misconceptions about Black women in American popular culture. One should be wary of the perception that these images are innocuous in nature. Canons both shape and reflect our perception of the world. Underscoring the relevance of popular culture especially that of these demeaning stereotypes, Black intellectual Michele Wallace argues that cultural criticism is as relevant as any other axis such as politics, the law, health, economics and the family to the lives and condition of Black women. Black women's empowerment, especially their ability to reclaim control over their lives, is inextricably linked with their artistic representations both by themselves and by the dominant hegemonic structure.

It is a relief that Storm is not constructed as the Negro spiritual woman, but her sexuality is completely absent because Hollywood is unwilling to offer her even the little representation that the comics did. In the comics she has some mobility, some agency, and most of all, the adoration of her people. Hollywood is clearly unwilling to offer this to Storm. Having two white men (Wolverine and Scott) fight over Jean Gray makes sense if you understand that to give Storm sexuality is to open up the conversation around what freedom looks like for Black women. If Storm can fall in love, then she can have children, and a life outside of the one Xavier of the films wants for "his" mutants.

This explains the missing Black man. Where the hell is he? Only one Black male character shows up in the films with Storm (Lucas Bishop played by Omar Sy), but the encounter set in a post-apocalyptic world and there is no backstory for either character. Research on that is beyond the scope of this book, but considering the construction of Storm in the films does offer a small explanation for the mostly absent Black man. Perhaps one of the reasons he is missing is because this opens the possibility of a love interests for her, and the creators do not want to make a space for a Storm free from the magical Negro and the mammy. A relationship would make her an actualized "person," not just a character designed to uphold white supremacy. The comics address this by giving her a backstory as a goddess, Black Panther as a lover, and other people that love and revere her. In the comics she is not forgotten, not used to make ice for a white man and his girlfriend, and she makes it rain for her community to live and thrive. Although she unrealistically leaves Kenya to follow Xavier, to have had and known love makes for a wholly different character than the one within the films. She has agency in the sky of Africa that she controls and bends to her own and her people's needs. There is freedom in this—even if it is limited.

Now the real question: Is bad representation of Black female sexuality better or worse than no representation at all? The answer, quite simply, is no. Bad representation is harmful, while no representation is equally, if differently, harmful. The films found it so easy to misrepresent Storm because in many ways the comics set up the blueprint. Suggesting that a Black woman is not "Negroid" because she is just barely good enough to be acceptable to white America is a violent construction against the bodies of Black women that do not look like Storm.

Black women and other minorities are told that they should be grateful for any representation and to toe the line, much as Storm has done throughout both the films and the comics. To expect this gratitude of Black women is, then, to become Xavier, who controls and dominates Black women into silence and submission, becoming the ultimate bad guy. The only difference between you and Xavier in that moment is that you, dear reader, are real.

Speaking, very unfortunately, of Xavier:

Having rewatched this series more than I care to admit over the last year, it is clear that Xavier is the villain of this series. He treats the mutants, the oppressed group, as if he owns them, and they are enslaved to him. Xavier is not the subject of this book, but he simply cannot be ignored. He gives speeches, claiming to be pro-mutant, but puts mutants in danger constantly. If the analogy of mutants representing Blackness is sound, Xavier spends the series abusing Black and marginalized bodies while forcing them to engage in their own oppression and support of white supremacy. He has committed a series of unforgiveable crimes against mutants, including exploiting the damaged children in his charge for his school gain, gaslighting the women around him, and he literally get mutants killed (the women, Jean Gray and Mystic, are perfect examples of his crimes). The only reason the film version of Professor X has not killed Storm is because the white creators need her body to maintain the illusion of inclusion in support of whiteness.

If beautiful, strong Storm can accept the world as it is, then why, Black woman, can't you?

6

Conclusion

• •

Are All Our Heroes Dead?

The first panel of the comic depicts a Black woman. She carries a machete in each hand, and her skin and her afro are black, smooth, and perfect. She is adorned with jewels, and her face is completely covered with a veil of shining stones, obscuring her face so that you will never know what she looks like. And, really, this is the point. She wears a necklace of jewels that drapes over her breast but the only clothing on her body is a long, multicolored, flowing loincloth to honor the ancestors. Her favorite colors are red, purple, and copper.

The text bubble tells you that this is Oya,[1] the ruler of death, the keeper of the last breath you take before you die. She is one of the first wives of Ogun, a warrior and powerful spirit in many African traditional religions (ATRs), including Yoruba traditions. That is, she is Ogun's wife until Chango, the Yoruba Orisha[2] of fire, lightning, thunder, and war, woos her. The subsequent panel shows Oya and Chango in an affectionate embrace, deeply in love, and partnered. She is Chango's second wife, and immediately upon arrival, Oya asserts her dominance in the house, as the bubble assures you that she needs to always be in control.

Being her normal inquisitive self—"nosy," the comic tells you—she finds a pot sitting on a podium in the middle of a dimly lit room. Because this is a classic comic, the depiction of the pot is massive, and she is shadowed in its presence. Oya is curious and investigates, tasting the liquid inside. "BAM!" the comic bubble reads. This is the magic that Chango uses to give him power over lightning and thunder. In the proceeding images, Oya symbolically grows larger and larger until she is bigger and more powerful than life. With this, Oya has gained the power to reign over lightning, leaving her almost as powerful as Chango himself. By gaining lightening, she gains control over Chango, as lightning and thunder must go together, tying him to her forever.

Oya becomes the decision maker, taking her place by Chango's side in battles and war. Chango does not make decisions without her, and she convinces him to pit his generals against each other hoping to kill them, to eliminate the threat they cause to her. One survives and he is so angry that he banishes them both from the kingdom. Chango is embarrassed and hangs himself from a tree, which is the moment he transitions from human form to an Orisha. Following him in life and death, Oya drowns herself in the Niger River where she also transitions into an Orisha.

But death is not the end for true deities. Now an Orisha, Oya reigns over storms. She is unpredictable, random, and powerful. Oya and Chango still fight in war together, using her power over lighting "to help [Chango] fight in his battles" (Edwards and Mason 93).

The next panel depicts a young child standing and looking into the distance, where she sees a water buffalo. In the sky is Chango, creating thunder, announcing the arrival of his beloved Oya. She appears carrying a lightning bolt that she uses as a whip to light up the sky. The girl cannot see her face but knows who the woman is instantly. She is afraid, because Oya can be violent and destructive as her grandmother has told her many times in the past, but her community desperately needs rain and *protection*, and Oya is a welcomed sight. One generally does not pray to Oya for monetary things, so the girl simply asks her hero for protection as Oya uses her great powers to flood the lands.

In the proceeding aftermath, the girl and her community are safe. But images portray great destruction and death. The military force that had invaded the region has been wiped out, not a man left alive; their guns and broken bodies litter the comic panel. The script reads: "For as far as the eye can see, *blood* on the land as warning for those who would seek to harm to *her* people."

More will come and bigger and better fights will follow, but Oya will always be there, protecting, avenging, and destroying to make way for new things to grow in her wake. In the next panel there are no people at all. They are not relevant. Oya herself is not necessarily relevant either. Instead, she has made way for the beginning of new things, growth, and prosperity for the people that need her most. There is a single red flower blooming, opening to the sky, looking in the direction of its mother, Oya, one of the most powerful deities in African traditional religions. These are the opening scenes to the comic whose story will follow the great Oya, queen of storms, new life and beginnings.

The account of these deities varies depending on which ATR is being honored. In some traditions she is never human, and in others Chango never hangs himself. Sometimes she controls thunder while Chango (also spelled Shango or Sa'ng'o) controls the lightening, and thus she precedes him, giving permission for him to strike, while controlling when and where the battle is fought. Often, too, she rules over the underworld, leading spirits through the darkness. The point, though, is that these deities are anchored to their communities and are beneficial for the members in that community. After all, what is a superhero if not a constructed deity?[3] Within the pages of comics and the images in films, people worship superheroes, just as they do deities, and place great faith in them to protect humanity. They are like gods. So, too, is the money that they bring to their creators, as in our society money is god and capitalism is religion.

Oya, on the other hand, cannot be bought and you cannot seek monetary gain from her to enrich yourself off her back or at the expense of other people. You cannot tell her to stand down or cower to a more powerful force because there are precious few forces that are more powerful than the true mother of storm, Oya. Moreover, she does not answer to the will of white men who want to keep the peace. She is uncontrollable, and this is important, as it does not allow her to be contained. She is loved by her man, Chango, despite her flaws and anger and rage. And she is given the space to have those flaws. She is in essence the god, deity, and hero for the people who need her the most. Authors Gary Edwards and John Mason, describe Oya as such:

[Oya] is associated with the sweeping winds of change and represents the forecaster for a point woman of change. She is invisible, dividing the line which foretells the change of the seasons, areas of strong wind movement and areas of dead calm, and the change of a person from being alive to being dead, that is represented by the person's last breath. Oya is represented by revolution and can be viewed as the power of progression or the power of reversal. . . . Her association with storms goes farther. Oya is the strong wind which precedes a thunderstorm, and it is said that when [Chango] wants to fight he sends Oya ahead of him to fight with her winds. It is further stated that without Oya there is nothing [Chango] can accomplish. Oya is the heavy, dark cloud which brings no rain. (92)

Oya is change. She is destructive and will destroy everything but will spare your life—because she is neither good nor evil, leaving you space to recreate your life bigger and better than before. You cannot bargain with her, as your fate is what you have earned and not what you can purchase. Weather can change the landscape, which in turn changes your fortune and future. Being originally in power over the last breath one takes, and thus death, she is also the guide to see you through that final transition of change. She is multifaceted and complicated, not simple and relevant.

Oya is the hero Black women deserve, while Storm is the one white people want to give us—or perhaps she is their gift to themselves. Within the X-Men, particularly the films, the white men around Storm can be flawed and violent and the white women, likewise, can be imperfect and vicious but Storm herself must occupy the space of perfection for her Black body to be a worthy superhero for white supremacy.

While this is a fun example of how Black female characters and heroes can be imagined within the context of this book's framework, there are Black women who are writing and creating amazing, powerful Black women characters. Examples are N. K. Jemisin's *Far Sector, Jennifer's Journal: The Life of a SubUrban Girl* by Jennifer Cruté, and Eve L. Ewing's *Ironheart*. There are more, and I highly recommend searching out and reading comics by and about Black women heroes.

Other Black Women's Theoretical Frameworks

This book has examined the relationship between Storm, Black feminist thought, and Patricia Hill Collins's controlling images of the mammy and jezebel. The conversation has also extended to include the magical Negro as simply a newer incarnation of a controlling image. All of these expand to the Negro spiritual woman, which includes Black women's sexuality. Looking at the "funnies" in this way is relevant because, as mentioned previously, Storm's sexuality has been constantly manipulated from her incarnation. Storm is simultaneously considered to be influential and one of the most powerful mutants in the X-men universe. This book has sought to discover whether Storm can maintain this perceived power despite the existence of these controlling images and the insidious nature of white supremacy within our society.

Black feminist thought is a theory devoted to analyzing the ideas of Black women, focusing on issues related to the Black female experience. Scholars state, "Feminist research approaches center on and makes problematic women's diverse situations and the institutions that frame those situations" (Creswell 75). This book reveals that while in some cases Storm is subversive and uses her power to benefit herself and Black people, she is more often constructed as the mammy, jezebel, the magical Negro, and more importantly, the Negro spiritual woman. Likewise, even when these images are not present, other negative archetypes emerge for Storm and other Black women within these series. Storm is subjugated and controlled through these controlling images and other negative stereotypes.

While the Black feminist framework is central to this text, it would be remiss not to address a vital criticism of Black feminism, which, as scholar Kinitra Brooks states, is that "Black feminist literary theory has claimed to act as a sustained critical project of subverting the Western literary hegemony," but has simply reinforced the canon, adding acceptable Black women elite writers, while ignoring the "ghetto genres" such as science fiction, fantasy and horror (*Searching for Sycorax*, 45). Through respectability politics, Black feminist thought has worked to shut out Black women genre writers. Black feminist theory has arguably been less subversion and more integration.

As such, I want to briefly offer a womanist framework as well. Womanism offers positive explorations of Black femininity's connection to spirituality. In *The Womanist Reader*, edited by Layli Phillips, the author states: "Womanism is a social change perspective rooted in Black women's and other women of color's everyday experiences and everyday methods of problem solving in everyday spaces," and furthermore its "link to gender is the fact that the historically produced race/class/gender matrix that is Black womanhood serves as the origin point for a speaking position that freely . . . addresses any topic or problem" (Phillips xx). In other words, womanism is not only rooted in minority women's (particularly Black women's) "everyday" methods of problem solving, but Black women's matrices of oppression offer them a unique position of race, class, and gender to "speak out against" all oppression. While Black women use their voices to speak about Black women's oppression, as womanists we are uniquely equipped to address all forms of persecution, against all peoples.

There are five characteristics of womanism which are integral to the foundation of the theory and crucial to understanding both the theory and how it avoids the trap of reinforcing hegemonic modalities, which traditional Black feminism does not. These are: *mothering, self-care, mutual aid, standing in* and *flying-over*. Here I outline each characteristic, briefly examining them in relation to Storm and X-Men.

Of *mothering*, Phillips states "[m]otherhood as a Womanist method of social transformation, has its roots in African cultural legacies . . . however, must be dissociated from its purely biological connotation and even from its strictly gendered connotation. . . . As Ogunyemi explains, using examples from West African cultures, most germane here are the notions of spiritual mother (Osun or Chi/Ori), mother as oracle (Odu), childless mother (Mannywata) and community mother (Omunwa/Iyalode)" (Phillips xxix). The concept of *self-care* is the site where Black women engage in caring for themselves, when others often do not. Black women are regularly expected to mother and care for people within their community who are not their children. Enacting self-care means not losing oneself while honoring one's commitment to community. The third concept, *standing in*, means simply to "stand in" and speak for those who often cannot speak for themselves. It means working for a new vision, a new language, or something that changes the way Black and minority people are positioned in society. Although called "standing in," this position is hardly stagnant. It allows Black women the space to freely move and control the arenas of life they navigate. It allows flexibility and mobility. Sometimes none of this activism works and one must engage in *flying-over*, starting anew, moving beyond, to be whole[4] and complete. One can fly-over to allow others to continue the fight, or one can choose to do so to engage in self-care, but the overall objective is to understand when one has completed one's mission and thus should move on to more self-fulfilling endeavors.

Mothering within womanism is different from mammying. While mothering is not purely biological, it also does not exist as an extension of the white supremacist patriarchy. Mothering benefits the Black woman, the child, and the community. In X-Men, Storm is mammied because she offers free labor in support of white children but has no space for dark-skinned children such as Marisol. In the films, she has no life or love interest outside of the constraints of this role and has no real freedom at all.

Storm's power comes from the elements. When Storm is seen in outside spaces, it is always in support of the white power structure. Indoors, Storm does not have the same access to her powers; thus, by surrounding her with concrete and the constraints of brick and mortar, Xavier has effectively subdued her, reducing her to nothing more than a maid for whiteness.

Self-care is not even a part of Storm's understanding of who she is. Not a single revolutionary moment in self-care exists for the character. In the comics, she has moments alone, but they are often spent worrying or thinking about the white people around her. In the films, she doesn't have a single memorable moment alone. I could be mistaken about this, and am unwilling to delve back into the films for a tenth or twentieth time to prove it; this alone does show that if the moment exists, there is nothing groundbreaking about it. Storm cannot engage in self-care because, again, this would highlight the way she is expected to use her often broken Black body to support Xavier's idea of mutant freedom, in juxtaposition to Black freedom.

This leads us to "standing in," and speaking for those who often cannot do it for themselves. Well, Storm does this sometimes—often in Africa with the children and group she helps to care for. That alone does not make it womanist, however. A womanist stands in to help herself and her Black community; she is not the faux Martin Luther King that white people have rewritten to use to appease their guilt while deflecting the conversation away from protection for Black bodies. Storm's perceived standing in is not womanist in nature. It simply works to hold on to the image that she is good enough for acceptance in white society

Finally, Storm is absolutely never given the opportunity to fly-over, because this would set her free from white male control. For Storm to start anew, she would have to leave the X-Men and become a fully actualized person. This would mean no mammying, no jezebel, no magical Negro and especially no Negro spiritual woman. Those are the things that contain her, and her white and male creators are simply not going to give her up. Flying-over often means giving up the fight, but for Storm it could look like leaving the X-Men, starting her own school with her own ideologies and own mission. It could look like gathering all the mutants in Africa and other disenfranchised places and teaching about sustainability and resistance. In this new space, she could power the world, provide rain, and restructure the landscape. But this will not happen because white men and women's imagination can only visualize her in service to them, her masters. Flying-over for Storm could also mean taking to the skies and never landing—simply because she is tired and wants freedom. This is not likely to be her fate, however. Because what is the X-Men without a Black servant masked as a loyal supporter of white, male dominance?

As we can see, Storm is not constructed within a womanist framework, and trying to do so is not likely to provide the proper context for analysis. This does show, however, that there is more than one analytical framework designed by and for Black women, and that Storm does not fit within either of them. A simple explanation for this is that she has not been created or written by Black women. But also, she does not exist to benefit Black women. On the contrary, she exists (much like white women in the films and in comics in general—Wonder Woman, for instance) solely for the benefit of white men—and the white society.

Content Analysis and the Negro Spiritual Woman

Content analysis is used to conduct this examination of Storm. Content analysis posits that there is no inherent meaning to text and that content must be read, analyzed and interpreted by the viewer—in this case, me, the researcher. It relies on previous research of Black media images, stereotypes, and comic book characters, and using a Black feminist thought framework, "as [a] critical social theory [that] aims to aid African American women's struggles against intersecting oppressions" (Creswell 135). We have found:

- Storm is rarely subversive, especially when interacting with other Black and marginalized female characters.
- Storm displays the jezebel stereotype throughout the comic series, but this stereotype is mostly absent in the films, as her sexuality is contained completely on screen.
- Storm exhibits the image of the mammy within both the comics and the films.
- Storm is constructed as a magical Negro figure within both the comics and the films.
- Storm is very often displayed as a Negro spiritual woman figure within the comics but not the films, specifically because her sexuality is contained completely in the latter medium.

- Storm is subjugated in ways that do not fall completely under any of the previous controlling images, but that are still negative.
- Storm is not "free" and she likely never will be until she is re-envisioned by Black women creators, or at least by people who understand the Black female experience.

This research suggest that Storm is indeed controlled through stereotypical images and racism, even if these particular images (of the mammy, jezebel, magical Negro and the Negro spiritual woman) are not always present. Storm, as a Black superheroine, is obviously gendered and racialized; however, her powers give the appearance that she is equal to her other superheroes. *Hero Me Not* has shown that this is categorically not the case.

The Construction of Good Blackness

Movies become a substitute for information on race for those who have little interaction with Black people, as do comic books and other mediums. Going briefly back to author Samuel Delany's claim that Black people are rarely placed in scenes together for fear that they'll sneak off and plan a "takeover or revolution," it is also important to remember that Delany states that the absence of Black people is often meant to show they are content in subservient positions to whites.

That is no less true for Storm within the X-Men universe. Readers have followed this character on her journey through several series and films, but ultimately, she is a loner; her community, sexuality, and power having been stripped from her. Storm has been known to exterminate those who threaten the X-Men and she uses her powers to support them unwaveringly. Storm is considered a good guy because of these things. She is constructed as such, arguably, because her "goodness" does not challenge the status quo. Storm's presence therefore offers an easy ally for white supremacy, without the appearance of doing so. If good Black women such as Storm do not challenge race or gender dynamics within society, then neither should others. Goodness here also comes from her free labor. Just as a slave is expected to work happily and devotedly to their master, Storm is expected to do so as well. Like the mammy, Storm is given charge of the house and the children when the master, Xavier, is away, but must become demure and subservient again when he, or any other white man, returns.

The controlling images outlined in this book are a dominant factor in Storm's life. As Patricia Hill Collins suggests, controlling images function in society to maintain the status quo and to help normalize oppression by making it appear the oppressed person is content or that they actually need to be controlled (77). One image alone is not enough to control Black women and we see through Storm that each of these controlling images intersects within her life. Storm's body is "othered," her sexuality is on display for the white male characters in the comics, and her multiple nationalities (being an American and African) work simultaneously to subjugate her.

Within these interlocking identities, Storm is expected to fulfill the stereotypical roles that whites have created. Storm is one of the "good guys" because she is the mammy, the jezebel, the magical Negro and the Negro spiritual woman, and only if she accepts these imposed roles as her own. If her character refused to accept them, it is not hard to imagine that she would be seen as "aggressive" more than "sincere," as previous research suggests, and that she would be more likely to be seen negatively than positively (Glenn and Cunningham 136). A Black woman who, for instance, refuses to accept the writing on an ancient African wall that orders her to submit to white men, despite the need for her help in Africa, would not be considered equally "good." After all, who would even question the righteous path of the X-Men, who fight and die for humanity, "for all of us," and society as it stands? Storm is simply constructed to see *the bigger picture* of whiteness, instead of the *micro-focus* of Blackness and Black people. This was the point of her teachings from Xavier.

Reiterating Dorothy Roberts's argument that the "social order established by powerful white men was founded on two inseparable ingredients: the dehumanization of Africans on the basis of race and the control of women's sexuality" (23), Storm's African identity is dehumanized, and she is controlled through her sexuality within both the comics and the films. However, the "myth" of our racial resistant culture, as Maurice Berger explains, tells us that "everything is all right," that these issues are not, and should not be present in Storm's life (92). Instead, the reader is shown that although mutantphobia exists, racism and sexism are just things of the past, not important to acknowledge in a functioning society any longer. Through this research, we see that this is not the case for Storm—despite the fact that the reader is led to believe that Storm is not only content with her life, but that this is her proper place, that she is destined to be subservient to the white male patriarchy.

Stereotypes cannot be removed from the construction of Black characters, and this is no different for comic book characters, including Storm. As a controlling image, the magical Negro specifically seeks to contain Black characters whose supernatural ability is so strong that it threatens the dominant group, but the Negro spiritual woman does so specifically because her sexuality is conceptualized as dangerous and detrimental for her and others. As such, being one of the most powerful mutants in the X-Men universe, Storm's ability to control the weather, both here on Earth and throughout the universe, marks her as unstable. Containing Storm through her sexuality and unimagined power, the NSW becomes a necessary stereotype which allows the white creator to maintain control over her, but it also allows audiences not to feel threatened by her. As a Black woman who is both African and African American, Storm is always walking a fine line that favors her Americanness over any part of her African identity. Thus, Storm does not question the racism in the United States or reject white supremacy, because this would bring attention to Blackness and thus her powers would instantly become volatile, a possible weapon against the very system that she was created to support.

Her containment as the Negro spiritual woman is as devastating for Storm as any of the other controlling images. The NSW, however, cannot be removed or separated from the other controlling images in any meaningful way. Instead, the NSW is a continuation, an extension of Patricia Hill Collins's controlling images, rather than being simply a unique entity all its own, much like the MN.

Wonder Woman as Predecessor

In some ways Storm has one of the best-known histories in all the X-Men universe. In other ways she is very much like Wonder Woman in that she has a "secret history" (Lepore). Wonder Woman is often depicted fighting for "justice, peace, and sexual equality," while because of her race, Storm is only free to fight for two of these, neither of which represent her full identity or her community. Storm's sexuality, however, is never free for her to wield. Like the function of "race" within Storm's life, to identify as sexual would expose the sexual politics behind Black women's bodies. Within the comic series, Storm's Black body is placed on display for white men to ogle, as she arguably relinquishes control of her own sexuality in a way that often

Wonder Woman does not. Likewise, Wonder Woman is an Amazonian princess in a matriarchal society, and thus she earns her powers and must prove herself to a female-led society. On the other hand, Storm's powers are often seen as volatile, and the act of sex with a man thrusts her into womanhood. While Storm has the freedom to choose her sexual partners, her femininity and her ability to control her powers is dependent on the power between her legs.

Storm does not have to prove herself through a compilation of physical challenges as Wonder Woman does, and she also is not free from sexual subjugation. She is not offered freedom over her own body or granted the latitude to learn about her own powers without having been taught to do so by a man. This containment of Storm's sexuality allows readers to accept her hero status as fully developed, but as subjugated and even controlled by patriarchy. She is not a threat to white America, and this is the point.

The comic reader does not question Storm's right to be a superhero because sex made her a woman and the love of a man made her more powerful. She is wholly contained and not likely to subvert the power structure. Unfortunately, while Wonder Woman has "limited agency," Storm is controlled completely through her sexuality and other controlling images (O'Reilly 273).

Scholars suggest that there are different levels of acceptance for men and woman, and for Black people and whites, within comic books and that is doubly so for Storm who is a Black woman with blue eyes and white hair. Not only does she have to prove that she can control herself and her powers, but she also must prove that she accepts the destiny of subordination to white rule before she can take true leadership within at least two of the three series and the films as well.

Like Wonder Woman, Storm's nationality is a subject of contention for her. Unlike Wonder Woman, Storm's body is not adorned in the American flag to prove where her true loyalties lie, but instead Storm's Black body itself is where this contention lies. Storm's Black skin is an obvious indicator that she is an outsider, an "other" within a world of the white supremacist capitalist patriarchy. As such, Storm struggles with reconciling her Africanness with her Americanness. Like all superheroes, Storm is supposed to represent her national loyalty above all others, as, say, Wonder Woman and Capitan America do. But considering intersectionality and examining the texts, one wonders what national loyalty is for Storm: her Africanness, her Americanness, her womanhood, her sexuality, her race, her gender? How does Storm reconcile all these things and still support the white power structure that is the X-Men over all others? How should she decide among them? Is it fair to expect her to do so?

We must conclude that the Black female superhero, Storm, is not offered sexual freedom, and is oppressed by her race in a way that her white female counterparts, such as Wonder Woman, Rogue, and Jean Gray, are not. Likewise, she seems to be contained and controlled through both her sexuality and her gender in a way that Black male superheroes, such as Black Panther, are not. This research also suggests that Storm's powers do not offer her freedom from subjugation and do not offer other Black female characters liberation through her appearance. Instead, as previous scholarship has suggested, Storm is often contained fully by her gender and race, and her superhuman powers do little to abate that subjugation (Spade and Valentine xv).

While it is arguable whether the depiction of Storm is sometimes subversive for her character, her sexual construction is colored by her identity as a Black woman in a white patriarchal society. More importantly, when subversive images are too abundant, other Black female characters are often subjugated in her stead. In this way, Blackness, Black female sexuality, and independence are fully contained and Storm is only left to identify with the white power structure, so as not to upset the status quo.

Ultimately, Storm is the creation of white imagination, like other controlling images, so she is too often not offered the autonomy or the ability to fully fight for the rights of her people, those of African or African American descent, as other superheroes are. Instead, Storm offers whites a docile image that is nonthreatening, and that easily fits into one of many stereotypes for which they are familiar. Keeping this in mind, it's very possible that Storm's creators imagined her in the only way they knew how: through mythical tropes of controlling images. When Storm supports the power structure it is not because she represents the very best that we believe we can be, but because she threatens the mostly white male power structure otherwise.

The Power of Storms and Oya

Going back to Orishas and the powerful figures in Black and other cultures that fight for and to benefit of the people who look like them, it is imperative that you understand that change is a constant and enduring force of a storm. Storms create new things, change landscapes, and foster conditions for growth that may not have otherwise been available. Storms are not stagnant. They cannot be such to be the powerful forces that they are. This means that the Storm of the X-Men is a direct antithesis of not only Oya, or the Storm of Orisha faith, but also of natural storms that happen around this globe multiple times a day. The Storm of the films does not change, grow, or evolve throughout the nearly twenty years of the film series. This means that the white creators of the character had to subvert the entire meaning of her name to make her fit into their narrative.

For humanity, there is no greater change than death. It is the most major transition that any of us will ever undergo in our entire lives, no matter your beliefs or ideologies. You go from a state of physical form to either not existing or, depending on your faith, to another plane of existence. In this, Oya has control over the last breath you take before you die, helping you to transition into whatever change is destined for you. She is there to ease you through the evolution that your body and spirit must undergo, and thus she is also the gatekeeper of the cemetery. That makes her one of the most fearless female Orishas in existence. She charges into battle and stands side by side with male Orishas, not seeking permission or affirmation from those men. She has weapons she took from Ogun, which is why she is almost always depicted with a pair of machetes in her hands. Add this to the elixirs she took from Chango to give her the power over thunder, lightning, or both, depending on the ATR in which she is worshiped, she is that "bad bitch" everyone hopes to see when they purchase a ticket for the next disappointing X-Men film. Oya is everything that Storm from X-Men could never be, everything that whiteness cannot imagine in a free Black woman—and specifically, cannot imagine lest they lose control of the Black female body through the rage they fear will consume them.

Acknowledgments

There are so many people that I want to acknowledge. If I forget someone, it is because my brain is in shambles at this point in the process and not because I do not value you for the support you have given me. Thanks, first, to my family, the most amazing support system that I could ever dream to have: Annie, Jerome, Jete, Brooke, Essence, Trinity, Carlanda, Chaka, Chad, Shad, and Josh who are always willing to listen and give me the space and time I need to discover who I am, and the latitude to screw up. To my soul sister, Monica Morris, for the debates, the deep discussions and passion that only comes from love. Thanks to my ancestors and my spiritual mother, father and sisters, Iya Karen (Shangotiti Layo) Daley-Onabamiro, Tata Raphael Santa, Sherise, Nicole, Amber, and Jose', the world would be much worse without you all. To Dr. Willie Tolliver, one of the most amazing academics I know, for the hours that I spent in your office, the high level of scholarly discourse, and the way you always encouraged me to value my own voice, ideas, and self, when others tried to silence me. Thanks, also, to Mikki Kendall and the amazing women of Black Phone, for the support and the hours I spent with you all online over the last decade. Maurice Broaddus, the writer, my friend, a treasure. To Dr. Dhanashree Thorat, who spent hours talking with me and walking me through finishing my PhD and dissertation (on Black girl magic), sending me gifts and feeding both my soul and scholarship. Thank you to the most amazing and all-around awesome person and friend, Rosalyn Monroe. Dr. Presley, thank you so much for opening your door to me during times of frustration while working on my "funnies." To Reverend Dr. Debra Walker King and Dr. Yvonne D. Newsome, thank you for always being the voices of reason. Thanks to my kickass editors Nicole Solano, Michelle Scott, and Donna Miele. Thank you, Dr. Makungu Akinyela, for being there during a difficult time, offering sound suggestions, and stepping up when this was just a thesis. Samuel R. Delany, you are a brilliant, thoughtful man who is always willing to share your knowledge with the younger generation, and I cannot thank you enough for that. Thanks, also, to Dr. Maurice Hobson and Dr. Jonathan Gayles.

Glossary

Black superhero A superhero who identifies as Black, African American, or within the African diaspora.

Black superheroine A superhero who both identifies as Black, African American, or within the African diaspora and as a woman.

Comics For the purpose of this book, "comics" is defined as comic strips that originated in the United States around the 1930s and mostly appeared in newspapers around the country.

Comic book Comic books are books (usually paperback) which consist of graphic art panels, short prose, dialogue, and narrative.

Comic book movies Comic book movies are movies, such as *Man of Steel*, which are based on comic book characters or plots.

Gender For the purposes of this book, I define gender as the social and cultural characteristics that distinguish men and women in society.

Genre For the purposes of this book, I define genre as works (literature, comics, music, images, film, and so on) that deal with the fantastic, such as science fiction, horror, fantasy, superheroes, etc.

Mutant In the comic book world, mutants are human beings who have extraordinary powers, and thus are "mutated" people.

Mutantism For the purposes of this book, mutantism is defined as being a mutant or having mutant powers.

Mutantphobia As defined in this research, mutantphobia is bigotry against mutants.

Patriarchy For the purposes of this study, the researcher defines patriarchy as a society in which men are dominant over women.

Race For the purposes of this research, the researcher defines race as Webster's dictionary does: a social concept used to categorize humans into large and distinct populations or groups by anatomical, cultural, ethnic, genetic, geographical, historical, linguistic, religious, and/or social affiliation.

Racism For the purposes of this book, I define racism as the sociologist, Yvonne Newsome does: a system and ideology of racial domination and exploitation that (a) incorporates beliefs in a particular race's cultural and/or biological inferiority and (b) uses such beliefs to justify and prescribe inferior or unequal treatment for that group. Racism embodies dual characteristics. It is both intuitional and attitudinal.

Sexism For the purposes of this book, I define sexism as the behaviors, attitudes, beliefs, customs, and intuitional practices that discriminate based on one's gender.

Stereotype For the purposes of this book, I define stereotype as the sociologist, Yvonne Newsome does: a one-sided, rigid, exaggerated, and prejudiced image or view of a group or class of people that is usually associated with racism, sexism, classism, etc.

Superhero I define superhero as Peter Coogan does: a heroic character with a selfless, prosocial mission; with superpowers . . . who has a superhero identity embodied in a codename or iconic costume.

Superheroine Superheroine is defined as a superhero who identifies as a woman.

Superpowers Extraordinary abilities, advanced technology, or highly developed physical, mental, or mystical skills.

Notes

Preface

1   Colorism, as argued by law professor Taunya Banks, is "skin tone discrimination against dark-skinned but not light-skinned blacks, [and] constitutes a form of race-based discrimination" (1705).
2   See further discussions on colorism in chapter 5.
3   In an interview with *Glamour*, Shipp dismisses the conversation around colorism and Storm's previous dark-skinned depictions as "Crayola from 1970" (Fitzsimons).
4   In an interview, bell hooks said she coined the term "white supremacist capitalist patriarchy" to provide "language that would actually remind us continually of the interlocking systems of domination that define our reality" in relation to race, gender, and class (Media Education Foundation 7).

Chapter 1   Introduction

1   We must only assume this is similar to the War of Northern Aggression, which in laymen's terms is a white supremacist fantasy that purports the Civil War wasn't about slavery, but instead an aggressive campaign by a North that wanted to control the South.
2   In her book *Sister Citizen*, Dr. Melissa Harris-Perry states that the Strong Black Woman "image figures prominently in the idea of Black women as overpowering" (287).
3   Sookie mostly uses her powers to save vampires and is arguably little more than a feeding source for the vampire men who have sex with her.
4   In season 5, episode 7, Patrick says to Terry: "Suicide is for Muslims, and you're better than that. You're a goddamn U.S. Marine"—proving that racism and bigotry is not reserved for Black people in Bon Temps, Louisiana.
5   For example, in season 5, episode 5, Pam chokes Tara in front of everyone in the bar and commands her never to attack a customer in sight of others. The problem here is

not that Tara shouldn't have been chastised, but that she is routinely treated more harshly than others have been in the past (Jessica didn't receive this treatment when she killed three of Andy Bellefleur's fairy daughters, for instance) and to add to the insult, Pam puts Tara in her place by telling her she is not worth as much as the bar.

6 Uppity is often a term leveled against Black people when they are perceived as not knowing their place. Its racial connotations go back to slavery and it was used by white Southerners against Black people who were often whipped or hanged for the offense.

7 Much in the same way as Halle Berry and Alexandra Shipp do in X-Men films.

8 Head N——In Charge. See, e.g., Urban Dictionary.

Chapter 2 Sexuality, Subjugation, and Magical Women

1 As a reminder "genre" is any category of work with similar themes and ideas, but in this book, I specifically refer to "genre" or "the genre field" as science fiction, fantasy, horror, comics, or any work with a speculative theme.

2 During his appearance at Yale, Spike Lee "cited four films in which there is a 'magical, mystical Negro' character: *The Family Man*, *What Dreams May Come*, *The Legend of Bagger Vance* and *The Green Mile*" (Yale Bulletin & Calendar).

3 In D. W. Griffith's movie *The Birth of a Nation* (1915), which is based on Thomas Dixon's novel *The Clansman* (1905), the mammy character is played by a white man in blackface makeup. As with most mammy caricatures, the character is masculine (as she is played by a man), dark (dark because of blackface makeup), fat, and unattractive, and she is sexually promiscuous.

4 Davy Jones is a reference to Davy Jones Locker, which is an idiom for the bottom of the sea, or where drowned sailors and shipwrecks go to their death. Therefore, Davy Jones himself is the man at the bottom of the sea who is responsible for those lost souls and ships. He is depicted as both calm and violent, as he is often considered the embodiment of the sea itself. The earliest known description of Davy Jones was published in 1751 by Tobias Smollett in *The Adventures of Peregrine Pickle:* "This same Davy Jones, according to sailors, is the fiend that presides over all the evil spirits of the deep, and is often seen in various shapes, *perching among the rigging on the eve of hurricanes*, ship-wrecks, and other disasters to which sea-faring life is exposed, warning the devoted wretch of death and woe" (emphasis added).

5 The goddess Calypso, originally spelled Kalypso, is a Greek Goddess and the daughter of Atlas. Calypso was considered beautiful although she could take any form she chose. She ruled over all of the seas and could control the sailors and ships within it. The sailors both loved and feared her, as she was, like Davy Jones, considered both violent and calming. Although Calypso could take many forms, the crab became her symbol in the legend. Calypso appeared in *The Odyssey* as a nymph who trapped Odysseus on her island so that he would eventually marry her.

6 Like most clichéd Black Hoodoo princesses on film, Dalma reads the future through mystical charms in a small hut on what resembles a haunted cinematic depiction of the Louisiana Bayou. Unlike others who have used rocks or other trinkets, Dalma uses crab claws to see the future—more than likely because she is from the sea or because crabs give her special power (later, she will turn into a legion of crabs). In this scene Dalma shakes the claws in her cupped hands and then throws them on the table, as if they were a pair of dice. The scene instantly

shifts to another location in the ocean, where the sea rocks are laid out in the exact pattern in which the crab claws had spread out on the table.

7 Speaking in a form of French Creole, Calypso curses the group of men on the ship, saying: "Malfaiteur en Tombeau, Crochir l'Esplanade, Dans l'Fond d'l'eau!" Translated, the phrase means: "To your graves, wrongdoers, I bend your path, to the depths of the sea!"

8 Examples of this are when Kee reveals her pregnancy to Theo in the barn as Mary of Nazareth births Christ in a barn; British terrorists who support the refuges are called "Fishes"; and critics such as Dana Stevens have called the movie a "modern-day Nativity story," comparing Theo and Kee to Joseph and Mary.

9 See the conversation on Black mothers and "mammying" in chapter 3.

10 In the movie, Hushpuppy's father tells her, "Show me them guns," and the girl proceeds to do a strong man pose, which consists of pumping her arms up and down, flexing her muscles.

11 In a 2011 study, "Racism and the Empathy for Pain on Our Skin," authors Matteo Forgiarini, Marcello Gallucci, and Angelo Maravita found that "Caucasian observers reacted to pain suffered by African people significantly less than to pain of Caucasian people. The reduced reaction to the pain of African individuals was also correlated with the observers' individual implicit race bias. The role of others' race in moderating empathic reactions is a crucial clue for understanding to what extent social interactions, and possibly integration, may be influenced by deeply rooted automatic and uncontrollable responses."

Chapter 3   The "Funnies" as a Discipline

1 Black people had always resisted enslavement, but rebellions such as Nat Turner's made it impossible to ignore.

2 Due to the Three-fifths Compromise, Black people were only considered three fifths of a person until 1868.

3 Movies from 1949's *Battleground* to the more modern *Saving Private Ryan*, which debuted in 1998, have used this model, Delany asserts.

4 One such book, Delany explains, is Heinlein's *Star Beast*, which has a Black female character best friend for the main white male lead in 1954, before desegregation. Email to author.

Chapter 4   Storm: The Comics

1 "Strange Fruit," as sung by Billy Holiday in 1939, refers to Black bodies hanging from trees because they have been lynched by white mobs.

2 Although later revised, the 1966 Book of Mormon written by Bruce R. McConkie states: "As a result of his rebellion [against his brother and god], Cain was cursed with a dark skin; he became the father of the Negroes, and those spirits who are not worthy to receive the priesthood are born through his lineage. . . . Negroes in this life are denied the priesthood; under no circumstances can they hold this delegation of authority from the Almighty (Abr. 1:20–27). . . . The Negroes are not equal with other races where the receipt of certain spiritual blessings are [*sic*] concerned, particularly the priesthood and the temple blessings that flow therefrom, but this inequality is not of man's origin. It is the Lord's doing" (McConkie 528).

3 It's important to note here that Darwin's scholarship is widely considered racist. Rasputin is brutal and uncompromising to his "children" and wants them to literally fight and kill each other so that only the best survives. This was written to play on the ideas of Darwin's survival of the fittest. There is a lot of research on the racism inherent in Charles Darwin's idea of evolutionary theory. John West, vice president and a senior fellow at the Discovery Institute states that Darwin's theory gave "a powerful push to a scientific version of racism that still impacts us today" (Borg).

4 Acknowledging here that Africa is a continent with fifty-four different counties and an untold number of cultures and peoples, the X-Men series often conflates Africans to one group, depicting them as a monolith.

5 "4C" is a classification of Black women's hair which is defined as tightly coiled, kinky, or both.

6 Coined by Black feminist scholar, writer, and activist Moya Bailey, "misogynoir" addresses the unique ways in which misogyny and racism impact Black women.

Chapter 5   Storm: The Films

1 The Free Dictionary defines the fourth wall in three ways:

    1 The imaginary barrier that is considered to separate the audience from the characters in a play or other live performance: *an actor who broke the fourth wall by directly addressing an audience member.*

    2 A similar imaginary barrier that is considered to separate a viewer from a film or other recorded performance: *traditional films that maintain the illusion of the fourth wall.*

    3 A similar imaginary barrier regarding as separating a text from its readers.

2 *Merriam-Webster's* dictionary says that the Bechdel Test is "a set of criteria used as a test to evaluate a work of fiction (such as a film) on the basis of its inclusion and representation of female characters. NOTE: The usual criteria of the Bechdel Test are (1) that at least two women are featured, (2) that these women talk to each other, and (3) that they discuss something other than a man."

Chapter 6   Conclusion

1 Ironically, Marvel has a character named Oya from Nigeria. Her powers include thermokinesis, pyrokinesis, and cryokinesis. Basically, she has the ability to alter temperatures, create fire, and make ice (yes, ice, again!). Other than creating fire and ice, Marvel's Oya bears little resemblance to the centuries-old Oya of Yoruba. Moreover, she is devoutly Catholic and believes she is a witch. Of course, in real life, Oya and those who worship her are considered witches specifically because of the teachings of Catholicism and other forms of Christianity.

2 Orisha "are deities [with] specific parts or forces selected to exist within God, [and] which govern different parts of the universe" (Edwards and Mason 1).

3 Think back to the discussion on American superheroes often being gods or having obtained their power from gods.

4 For the Womanist, being whole is not just physical, psychological, social, or even economic; it is also becoming spiritual and cosmologically unifying, reaching back to Sankofa and acknowledging one's ancestors.

Works Cited

Abdullah, Afi Samelia. "Mammy-ism: A Diagnosis of Psychological Misorientation for Women of African Descent." *Journal of Black Psychology* vol. 24, no. 2 (1998): 196–210.

Aiken, K. G. "Superhero History: Using Comic Books to Teach U.S. History." *OAH Magazine of History* vol 24, no. 2 (April 2010): 41–47.

Alter, Adam L., Chadley Stern, Yael Granot, and Emily Balcetis. "The 'Bad Is Black' Effect: Why People Believe Evildoers Have Darker Skin Than Do-Gooders." *Personality and Social Psychology Bulletin* vol. 42, no. 12 (2016): 1653–1665.

Arnold-Ratliff, Katie. "Anti-Racism for Kids: An Age-by-Age Guide to Fighting Hate." *Parents*, updated March 17, 2021, www.parents.com/parenting/better -parenting/advice/how-to-teach-your-kids-to-fight-hate-an-age-by-age-guide/.

Banks, Taunya Lovell. "Colorism: A Darker Shade of Pale." *UCLA Law Review* vol. 47, part 6 (2000): 1705–1746.

Beauboeuf-Lafontant, Tamara. *Behind the Mask of the Strong Black Woman: Voice and Embodiment of a Costly Performance.* Philadelphia: Routledge, 2009.

Beck, Laura. "The Only Oscar GIF You Need, Starring Quvenzhané Wallis." Jezebel, February 25, 2013, jezebel.com/5986598/the-only-oscar-gif-you-need-starring -quvenzhane-wallis.

Berger, Maurice. *White Lies: Race and the Myths of Whiteness.* New York: Farrar, Straus and Giroux, 2000.

Bordwell, David, and Kristi Thompson. *Film Art: An Introduction.* New York: McGraw Hill, 2012.

Borg, Julie. "Darwin's Racism: How Early Evolutionary Theory Fueled Discrimination." World, June 18, 2020, wng.org/roundups/darwins-racism-1617223432.

Brantlinger, Patrick. "Victorians and Africans: The Genealogy of the Myth of the Dark Continent." *Critical Inquiry* vol. 12, no. 1 (1985): 166–203.

Brooks, Kinitra. "Finding the Humanity in Horror: Black Women's Sexually Identity in Fighting the Supernatural." *Poroi* vol. 7, no. 2 (2011): 1–14, https://doi.org/10 .13008/2151-2957.1098.

————. *Searching for Sycorax: Black Women's Hauntings of Contemporary Horror.* Rutgers UP, 2018.

Brown, Kimberly Nichele. *Writing the Black Revolutionary Diva Women's Subjectivity and the Decolonizing Text.* Bloomington: Indiana UP, 2010.

Burke, Chesya. "Black Woman and the New Magical Negro." In *African American Cinema Through Black Lives Consciousness*, edited by Mark A. Reid. Detroit: Wayne State UP, 2019.

Burns, Sarah, Lindsey Eberhardt, and Jennifer Merolla. "What Is the Difference between a Hockey Mom and a Pit Bull? Presentations of Palin and Gender Stereotypes in the 2008 Presidential Election." *Political Research Quarterly* vol. 66, no. 3 (2013): 687–701. *JSTOR,* http://www.jstor.org/stable/23563175.

Carby, Hazel. *Reconstructing Womanhood: The Emergence of the Afro-American Woman Novelist.* New York: Oxford UP, 1989.

Cartwright, Samuel. "Report on the Diseases and Physical Peculiarities of the Negro Race." *New Orleans Medical and Surgical Journal*, May 1851: 691–715.

Chanliau, Pierre. "Former X-Men Actress Wants One Important Change for MCU's Storm." *The Direct*, March 11, 2022, thedirect.com/article/mcu-x-men-storm -actress.

Claremont, Chris. *Uncanny X-Men.* vol. 253 (Nov. 15, 1989). Marvel Comics.

Collins, P. H. *Black Feminist Thought, Knowledge, Consciousness, and the Politics of Empowerment.* New York: Psychology Press, 2000.

Collins, Suzanne. *The Hunger Games.* New York: Scholastic Press, 2008.

Combahee River Collective. *The Combahee River Collective Statement.* Mexico City: Gato Negro Ediciones, 2017.

Creswell, J. W., and Poth, C. N. *Qualitative Inquiry & Research Design Choosing among Five Approaches.* Thousand Oaks, CA: Sage Publications, 2018.

Cuarón, Alfonso, director. *Children of Men.* Strike Entertainment (2006).

D'Amore, Laura Mattoon. "The Accidental Supermom: Superheroines and Maternal Performativity, 1963–1980." *The Journal of Popular Culture* vol. 45, no. 6 (Dec. 2012): 1226–1248.

Daniels, Les. *Wonder Woman: The Complete History.* San Francisco: Chronicle, 2004.

Darowski, Joseph J. *X-Men and the Mutant Metaphor: Race and Gender in the Comic Books.* Ann Arbor, MI: Rowman & Littlefield Publishers, 2014.

Davis, Angelique M., and Rose Ernst. "Racial Gaslighting." *Politics, Groups, and Identities* vol. 7, no. 4 (2019): 761–774.

Davis, Brandon. "Dark Phoenix Star Alexandra Shipp Reveals Her Idea for a Storm Movie." ComicBook, May 23, 2019, comicbook.com/marvel/news/dark-phoenix -storm-alexandra-shipp-movie-halle-berry/.

Delany, Samuel R. *Silent Interviews on Language, Race, Sex, Science Fiction, and Some Comics: A Collection of Written Interviews.* Hanover, NH: Wesleyan UP, 1994.

Dickey, Eric Jerome. *Storm.* Series, #1–6. Marvel, 2006.

Dines, Gail, and Jean McMahon Humez. *Gender, Race, and Class in Media: Text Reader.* Thousand Oaks, CA: Sage Publications, 1994.

Duncan, Randy, and Matthew J. Smith. *The Power of Comics: History, Form and Culture.* New York: Continuum, 2009.

Edwards, Gary, and John Mason. *Black Gods—Òrìṣà Studies in the New World.* Yorùbá Theological Archministry, 1998.

Ellis, Warren. *Storm.* 1st series (the Gene Nation series), #1–4. Marvel Comics, 1996.

Emad, Mitra C. "Reading Wonder Woman's Body: Mythologies of Gender and Nation." *The Journal of Popular Culture* vol. 39, no. 6 (2006): 954–984.

Entman, R. M., and A. Rojecki. "The Entman-Rojecki Index of Race and the Media." In *The Black Image in the White Mind: Media and Race in America*. U Chicago P, 2000, press.uchicago.edu/Misc/Chicago/210758.html.

Fishman, Joshua A. "Childhood Indoctrination for Minority-Group Membership." *Daedalus* vol. 90, no. 2 (1961): 329–349.

Fitzsimons, Amanda. "Why Alexandra Shipp Won't Be Censored." *Glamour*, July 6, 2018, www.glamour.com/story/alexandra-shipp-wont-censor-herself.

Fonow, Mary. "Beyond Methodology: Feminist Scholarship As Lives Research." *Signs* vol. 30, no. 4 (2005): 2211–2236.

Forgiarini, Matteo, Marcello Gallucci, and Angelo Maravita. 2011. "Racism and the Empathy for Pain on Our Skin." *Frontiers in Psychology*, May 23, 2011, https://doi.org/10.3389/fpsyg.2011.00108.

Free Dictionary. www.thefreedictionary.com/.

Ganeshram, Ramin, and Vanessa Brantley-Newton. *A Birthday Cake for George Washington*. New York: Scholastic Press, 2016.

Gayles, Jonathan. "Black Macho and the Myth of the Superwoman Redux: Masculinity and Misogyny in Blade." *Journal of Popular Culture* vol. 45, no. 2 (2012): 284–300.

Gilkes, Cheryl. "From Slavery to Social Welfare: Racism and the Control of Black Women (1981)." In *Class, Race, and Sex: The Dynamics of Control*, edited by Amy Swerdlow and Hanna Lessinger. Boston: G. K. Hall, 1983.

Glenn, C. L., and L. J. Cunningham. "The Power of Black Magic: The Magical Negro and White Salvation in Film." *Journal of Black Studies* vol. 40, no. 2 (2009): 135–152.

Harris, Trudier. 1995. "Genre." *Journal of American Folklore* vol.108, no. 430 (1995): 509–527.

Harris-Perry, Melissa V. *Sister Citizen Shame, Stereotypes, and Black Women in America*. Yale UP, 2014.

Hetey, Rebecca C., and Jennifer L. Eberhardt. "The Numbers Don't Speak for Themselves: Racial Disparities and the Persistence of Inequality in the Criminal Justice System." *Current Directions in Psychological Science* vol. 27, no. 3 (2018): 183–187, https://doi.org/10.1177/0963721418763931.

hooks, bell. *Black Looks: Race and Representation*. Boston: South End Press, 1992.

———. *Killing Rage: Ending Racism*. New York: H. Holt, 1995.

———. "No Love in the Wild." New Black Man (in Exile), Sept. 5, 2012, newblackman.blogspot.com/2012/09/bell-hooks-no-love-in-wild.html.

Hughey, Matthew. "Cinethetic Racism: White Redemption and Black Stereotypes in 'Magical Negro' Films." *Social Problems* vol. 56, no. 3 (2009): 543–577.

IMDb. "X-Men (2000): Plot." www.imdb.com/title/tt0120903/plotsummary.

Kinberg, Simon. *X-Men: Dark Phoenix*. 20th Century Fox, 2019.

King, Deborah K. "Multiple Jeopardy, Multiple Consciousness: The Context of a Black Feminist Ideology." *Sign*, vol. 14, no. 1 (1988): 42–72.

King, Martin Luther, Jr. "Letter from Birmingham Jail." *Atlantic Monthly*, vol. 212, no. 2 (Aug. 1963): 78–88, www.csuchico.edu/iege/_assets/documents/susi-letter-from-birmingham-jail.pdf.

Krystal, Arthur. "It's Genre. Not That There's Anything Wrong with It!" *New Yorker*, October 24, 2012, www.newyorker.com/online/blogs/books/2012/10/its-genre-fiction-not-that-theres-anything-wrong-with-it.html.

Lepore, Jill. *Secret History of Wonder Woman*. New York: Knopf Doubleday Group, 2014.

———. "The Surprising Origin Story of Wonder Woman." *Smithsonian Magazine*, October 2014, www.smithsonianmag.com/arts-culture/origin-story-wonder -woman-180952710/.

Lorde, Audre. *Sister Outsider*. New York: Penguin Books, 2020.

Lynn, Cheryl. "Trinity: The Black fantasy." cheryllynneaton.com/2009/05/07/trinity -the-black-fantasy/.

Marvel Entertainment. "A Message from Stan Lee." YouTube video, Oct. 5, 2017, youtu.be/sjobevGAYHQ.

Marvel.com. "X-Men: Apocalypse." www.marvel.com/movies/x-men-apocalypse. Accessed July 20, 2022.

Mathews, Tayler J., and Glenn S. Johnson. "Skin Complexion in the Twenty-First Century: The Impact of Colorism on African American Women." *Race, Gender & Class* vol. 22, no. 1–2 (2015): 248–274.

McConkie, B. R. *Mormon Doctrine*. Salt Lake City, UT: Deseret, 1966.

McGrath, Karen. "Gender, Race, and Latina Identity: An Examination of Marvel Comics' Amazing Fantasy and Araña." *Atlantic Journal of Communication* vol. 15, no. 4 (2007): 268–283.

Means Coleman, Robin. *Horror Noire: Black People in American Horror Films From the 1890s to Present*. New York: Routledge, 2011.

Media Education Foundation. *bell hooks—Cultural Criticism & Transformation*. Edited by Mary Patierno, Sut Jhally, and Harriet Hirshorn, 1997. www.mediaed .org/transcripts/Bell-Hooks-Transcript.pdf.

Merriam-Webster, www.merriam-webster.com.

Morrison, Toni. *Playing in the Dark: Whiteness and the Literary Imagination*. New York: Vintage, 1995.

Nanda, S. "Re-Framing Hottentot: Liberating Black Female Sexuality from the Mammy/Hottentot Bind." *Humanities* 2019 vol. 8, no. 161 (2019), https://doi.org /10.3390/h8040161.

Nelmes, Jill. *An Introduction to Film Studies*. New York: Routledge, 1999.

O'Reilly, Julie D. "The Wonder Woman Precedent: Female (Super)Heroism on Trial." *Journal of American Culture* vol. 28, no. 3 (Sept. 2005): 273–283.

Oxford English Dictionary. "New Words List October 2019." https://public.oed.com /updates/new-words-list-october-2019/.

Pak, Greg. *Storm*, vols. 1–2. *Make It Rain / Bring the Thunder*. Marvel, 2015.

Peters, Brian Mitchell. "Qu(e)erying Comic Book Culture and Representations of Sexuality in Wonder Woman." *CLC Web: Comparative Literature and Culture* vol. 5, no. 3 (2003). https://docs.lib.purdue.edu/cgi/viewcontent.cgi?article =1195&context=clcweb.

Petty, John. *A Brief History of Comic Books*. Dallas: Heritage Auction Galleries. www.heritagestatic.com/comics/d/history-of-comics.pdf.

Phillips, L. *The Womanist Reader*. London: Routledge Taylor & Francis Group, 2006.

Pough, Gwendolyn, and Yolanda Hood. "Speculative Black Women: Magic, Fantasy, and the Supernatural." *Femspec* vol. 6, no. 1 (2005): ix.

Radford-Hill, Sheila. "Keepin' It Real: A Generational Commentary on Kimberly Springer's 'Third Wave Black Feminism?'" *Signs* vol. 27, part 4 (2002): 1083–1090.

Ratner, Bret, director. *X-Men: The Last Stand*. 20th Century Fox, 2006.

Roberts, Dorothy. *Killing the Blackbody: Race, Reproduction, and the Meaning of Liberty*. New York: Vintage Books, 1997.

Rose, Charlie. "Charlie Rose Interviews Toni Morrison." 19 Jan. 19, 1998.

Rosenberg, Robin S., and Jennifer Canzoneri. *The Psychology of Superheroes: An Unauthorized Exploration*. Dallas: Ben Bella, 2008.

Royal, Derek. "Visualizing the Romance: Uses of Nathaniel Hawthorne's Narratives in Comics." *Nathaniel Hawthorne Review* vol. 39, no. 2 (2013): 126–153.

Ryan, Jennifer. "Black Female Authorship and the African American Graphic Novel: Historical Responsibility in Icon: A Hero's Welcome." *MFS Modern Fiction Studies* vol. 52, no. 4 (2006): 918–946.

Saini, Anna. "Annals of the Black Superheroine." *Bitch Magazine: Feminist Response to Pop Culture* no. 42 (2009): 96.

Schumacher, Joel, director. *A Time to Kill*. Warner Bros., 1996.

Scott, Anna Beatrice. "Superpower vs. Supernatural: Black Superheroes and the Quest for a Mutant Reality." *Journal of Visual Culture* vol. 5, no. 3 (2006): 295–314.

Settles, Isis H., et al. "Through the Lens of Race: Black and White Women's Perceptions of Womanhood." *Psychology of Women Quarterly* vol. 32, no. 4 (2008): 454–468.

Singer, Bryan, director. *X-Men*. 20th Century Fox, 2000.

———, director. *X-Men: Apocalypse*. 20th Century Fox, 2016.

———, director. *X-Men: Days of Future Past*. 20th Century Fox, 2014.

———, director. *X2: X-Men United*. 20th Century Fox, 2003.

Singer, Marc. "'Black Skins' and White Mask: Comic Books and the Secret of Race." *African American Review* vol. 36, no. 1 (2002): 107–119.

Smith, Andrea. "Boarding School Abuses, Human Rights, and Reparations." *Social Justice* vol. 31, no. 4 (2004): 89–102.

Spade, Joan Z, and Catherine G. Valentine, eds. *The Kaleidoscope of Gender: Prisms, Patterns, and Possibilities*. 4th edition. Thousand Oaks, CA: SAGE Publications, 2014.

Speculative Literature Foundation. https://speculativeliterature.org.

Stevie, John. "Out of Character: Why the Latest Transformation of Wonder Woman Has Fans Concerned." *Bitch Magazine: Feminist Response to Pop Culture* 63 (2014): 28–33.

Sumerak, Marc. *Ororo: Before the Storm*. #1–4. Marvel, 2005.

Swanson, Jessica. "Sexual Liberation or Violence against Women? The Debate on the Legalization of Prostitution and the Relationship to Human Trafficking." *New Criminal Law Review: An International and Interdisciplinary Journal* vol. 19, no. 4 (2016): 592–639.

Trennert, Robert A. "Educating Indian Girls at Nonreservation Boarding Schools, 1878–1920." *The Western Historical Quarterly* vol. 13, no. 3 (1982): 271–90. *JSTOR*, https://doi.org/10.2307/969414.

True Blood. Alan Ball, creator. HBO series, 2008–2014. www.hbo.com/true-blood.

Verbinski, Gore. *Pirates of the Caribbean: At World's End*. Walt Disney Studios, 2007.

———. *Pirates of the Caribbean: Dead Man's Chest*. Walt Disney Studios, 2006.

Viglione, Jill, Lance Hannon, and Robert DeFina. "The Impact of Light Skin on Prison Time for Black Female Offenders." *Social Science Journal* vol. 48, no. 1 (2011): 250–258.

Wein, Len. *Giant-Size X-Men* #1. Marvel, 1975.

Windsor, Liliane Cambraia, Eloise Dunlap, and Andrew Golub. "Challenging Controlling Images, Oppression, Poverty, and Other Structural Constraints: Survival Strategies among African-American Women in Distressed Households." *Journal of African American Studies* vol. 15, no. 3 (2010): 290–306.

Yale Bulletin & Calendar. "Director Spike Lee Slams 'Same Old' Black Stereotypes in Today's Films." vol. 29, no. 2, March 2, 2001, archives.news.yale.edu/v29.n21/story3 .html.

Zeitlin, Benh. *Beast of the Southern Wild*. Fox Searchlight, 2012.

Index

Page numbers in *italics* represent images.

About the Author

CHESYA BURKE is an assistant professor of English and U.S. literatures and director of Africana Studies at Stetson University. Having written and published nearly a hundred fiction pieces and articles within the genres of science fiction, fantasy, comics, and horror, her academic research focuses predominantly on the intersections of race, gender, and genre. Her primary areas of study are in African American literature, race and gender studies, comics, and speculative fiction. Her story collection, *Let's Play White*, is being taught in universities around the world.